THE
FORTY-HOURS
DEVOTION
TO JESUS
IN THE
BLESSED
SACRAMENT

BLESSED AND PRAISED EVERY MOMENT
BE THE MOST HOLY AND DIVINE SACRAMENT
(Indulgence, 300 days, each time)

THE
FORTY-HOURS' DEVOTION
TO JESUS
IN THE BLESSED SACRAMENT

Its prayers and ceremonies explained for the special use of the Catholic people, so that they may attend and follow this devotion with understanding. To which are added Prayers and Readings for Two Half-Hour Visits to the Blessed Sacrament.

By

Rev. J. E. MOFFATT, S.J.

Author of "The Morning Sacrifice", etc.

With Illustrations After Special Drawings in Accordance With the Ceremonial of the Church.

BENZIGER BROTHERS

NEW YORK, CINCINNATI, CHICAGO
𝔅𝔢𝔫𝔷𝔦𝔤𝔢𝔯 𝔅𝔯𝔬𝔱𝔥𝔢𝔯𝔰
Printers to the Holy Apostolic See
1928

CONTENTS

———

𝕴𝖒𝖕𝖗𝖎𝖒𝖎 𝕻𝖔𝖙𝖊𝖘𝖙

    JOSEPH M. PIET, S.J.

        Praep. Prov. Californiae

𝕹𝖎𝖍𝖎𝖑 𝕺𝖇𝖘𝖙𝖆𝖙

    ARTHUR J. SCANLAN, S.T.D.

        Censor Librorum

𝕴𝖒𝖕𝖗𝖎𝖒𝖆𝖙𝖚𝖗

    ✠PATRICK, CARDINAL HAYES
        Archbishop of New York

NEW YORK, SEPTEMBER, 1, 1928.

INTRODUCTION

WHAT IS THE FORTY-HOUR DEVOTION Devotion to Jesus in the Holy Eucharist is the most beautiful and fruitful of all devotions. The whole life of the Church is centered about its Eucharistic God. The Adorable Sacrament of Love is the sacred fount whence flow streams of life-giving grace to the thirsting souls of men. It is the banquet board of the King whereat famished spirits are feasted and refreshed with the immaculate Flesh of the Lamb. Here too, the King of heaven holds His court, harkening to the pleadings of the needy and distressed, dispensing His mercy and His peace with infinite bounty.

Nor to the soul that loves Jesus with a generous love, is the Blessed Sacrament only a storehouse of treasures to be drawn from for its own enriching. It is this, indeed, but it is more. It is a living memorial of the Passion and death of the world's Redeemer, arousing in the soul a desire to make a return of love for love; stirring it up to repair the wrong it has done and to atone for the sins and insults of mankind.

To aid the faithful in their sacred duty towards their Eucharistic God, holy Mother Church has provided many inspiring forms of devotion. Outstanding amongst them all in the simple beauty of its ceremonial and the abundance of its spiritual fruitfulness, is the Forty-Hours' Adoration.

This beautiful devotion is celebrated in memory of the forty hours during which the sacred Body of Jesus reposed in the sepulchre. Enthroned amid lights and lilies, and surrounded by the adoring faithful, or carried in solemn procession amidst the joyful sound of sacred song borne heavenward from prayerful lips, or offered in holy Sacrifice upon the altar, Jesus the King of kings, receives the homage of His children, pleads their cause with His heavenly Father, and pours the riches of His precious grace into their needy souls.

ORIGIN OF THE DEVOTION   The origin of this inspiring devotion may be traced to the early part of the sixteenth century. The year 1527 saw the city of Milan in the throes of despair. Already terribly scourged by disease and famine, there now hung over it the added horror of threatened invasion by the imperial army which had recently sacked the city of Rome. In their extremity the people had recourse to prayer. Led by a holy priest, they gathered in the church, and there before the tabernacle, knelt in adoration, begging their hidden God to avert the impending evil. For forty consecutive hours groups of faithful adorers alternately kept their prayerful watch. Their prayer was heard; Milan was spared and peace was restored to its people.

Such was the beginning of this great devotion. At first it was marked by the utmost simplicity. No pomp or ceremony attended it. The Blessed Sacrament was not exposed, but the people adored before the tabernacle. Thus it continued for the first decade after its institution.

THE FOUR GREAT DOCTORS OF THE LATIN
CHURCH (St. Augustine, St. Jerome, St.
Ambrose and St. Gregory) and
THE HOLY EUCHARIST

Page 7

In the year 1537 Milan was again in a state of dire distress. Not only were there perils impending from without, but the moral degradation into which the people had fallen threatened to call down upon their unhappy heads the wrath of an angry God. In this new hour of peril, Fra Giuseppe da Ferno, a saintly Capuchin friar, appealed to the people to again have recourse to the Forty Hours' Prayer to win God's mercy. But he proposed to surround it with greater solemnity that it might do greater honor to the Most High. Accordingly the Blessed Sacrament was exposed for the adoration of the faithful; solemn processions were instituted, hymns and psalms were chanted, and every mark of exterior pomp and ceremony added to lend grandeur to the devotion.

Again the effect was marvelous. Not only was the city saved, but the spirit of paganism which was fast undermining the faith of the people, and wreaking its devastating influence upon society was checked and religion again became the all-important thing of life. The Eucharistic King was once again enthroned in the hearts of His people.

CHARACTERISTICS OF THE DEVOTION To appreciate more fully the true significance of the devotion, it will be well to note the characteristics which marked its origin. Begun in an hour of misery, it was a cry of distress of the human heart to God when earthly assistance proved of no avail; it was a prayer for peace when all was sorrow and unrest. It was also a penitential act; an humble atonement of sin to ward off the Divine wrath, and a sincere resolution of future amendment. No less was it a sacred memorial of the passion and death of the world's Redeemer; an awakening of a sense of loyalty to Christ by recalling all that He suffered for mankind.

SPREAD OF THE DEVOTION Fostered by the clergy, the devotion quickly spread to other cities of Italy, and in 1551, through the zeal of Saint Philip Neri, was established in Rome. Here, by an Apostolic Constitution of Clement VIII, dated Nov. 25, 1592, provision was made that exposition should be had in continuous succession in the different churches of the city.

Pope Paul V, in 1606, confirmed the Constitution of Clement VIII, and by a new Decree, established the Devotion in perpetuity. From time to time succeeding Pontiffs added regulations for the right ordering of the devotion, and in 1707, Pope Clement XI, having gathered and rearranged all that had been decreed by his predecessors, published his "Clementine Instruction," an elaborate ceremonial code wherein everything concerning the Forty Hours' Prayer is specified in detail. In the city of Rome this code is of strict obligation; elsewhere it serves as a directive norm or rule to be observed where possible.

INTRODUCTION INTO THE UNITED STATES In 1853, Bishop Neumann, of saintly memory, realizing the benefits to be derived

ST. THOMAS AQUINAS COMPOSING THE
OFFICE OF "CORPUS CHRISTI" FOR
THE BREVIARY

from so salutary a devotion, introduced it into the diocese of Philadelphia. Five years later, in 1858, it was begun in the Archdiocese of Baltimore, and at length, in 1866, the Plenary Council of Baltimore gave it formal approbation for all Dioceses of the United States. However, owing to conditions, it was deemed impossible to observe strictly all the details of the Clementine Instruction. Hence a petition was made to the Holy See by The Most Reverend F. P. Kenrick, Archbishop of Baltimore, asking that certain modifications be granted. In reply, the Holy Father, by a rescript dated December 10, 1857, made the following concessions to all the Dioceses of the United States: First—The Exposition of the Blessed Sacrament may be interrupted during the night. Second—In case of necessity, the procession may be omitted. Third—The faithful may gain all the indulgences granted to those who assist at the devotion when conducted strictly according to the Clementine Instruction.

A RICH DE- Since the first recognition of the
    VOTION   Devotion by the Church, various
Pontiffs have given it further encouragement by enriching it with holy indulgences, both Plenary, (full remission of the temporal punishment due to sin) and Partial, (remission of part of the temporal punishment due to sin). These Indulgences, applicable to the holy souls, are as follows:

A Plenary Indulgence to all who, after Confession and Communion, (in the church of Exposition or elsewhere) shall visit the Blessed Sacrament Exposed, on one of the three days, and pray for the intention of the Holy Father.

An Indulgence of ten years and ten times forty days, for every visit made with true contrition and a firm purpose of going to confession.

In the church where the Exposition takes place, all the altars are privileged, i.e., in addition to the ordinary fruits of the Eucharistic Sacrifice, a Plenary Indulgence is granted for every Mass offered on such altars.

HOW TO ASSIST AT THE DEVOTION To participate to the fullest extent in the fruits of this devotion, we must assist at it in a spirit of lively faith, of ardent love for our Eucharistic King, with true contrition for our own sins and the sins of the world, accompanied by a sincere purpose of amending our lives and atoning for our past infidelity. A complete renovation of spirit should be the result in each individual soul.

We must also bear in mind that the Prayer is a cry of the Church for her own needs and the needs of her children. Hence we must during this time awaken within our hearts a spirit of universal charity. This can be best accomplished by assisting at the Solemn Mass which marks the beginning of each day's ceremony; by following the sacred ritual with which the Devotion is surrounded; by participating (when the custom prevails) in the solemn processions and by joining fervently in the public prayers which are recited.

THE UNIVERSAL ADORATION OF THE
BLESSED SACRAMENT

Frequent visits to our Eucharistic Lord should also be made, if possible, during the hours of Exposition.

Thus shall the faithful soul, participating in the inspiring liturgical functions of this charming devotion, or kneeling in silent communion with our Adorable Saviour exposed in His Sacrament of Love, render to God an act of homage most pleasing to the Divine Majesty, and win for itself and the Church untold graces and blessings.

That this may be the better accomplished is the object of this little work. May our Eucharistic Saviour deign to bless it, and by its means, draw many souls to a deeper appreciation of His sweet Sacrament of Love.

J. E. MOFFAT, S.J.

HOLY THURSDAY 1928.

THE LITURGY
OF THE
FORTY-HOURS' DEVOTION

FIRST DAY

THE MASS The Ceremony begins with solemn Mass. The Mass of Exposition, celebrated on the first day, is, (rubrics permitting) the solemn Mass of the Blessed Sacrament. The vestments worn are white, this being the color proper to the Blessed Sacrament. (In case of necessity a low Mass may be celebrated.)

THE ORDINARY OF THE MASS

The people stand when the celebrant and his ministers enter the Sanctuary.

THE BEGINNING *Standing at the foot of the altar, the celebrant* **OF MASS** *begins with the sign of the Cross; the deacon* **Kneel** *and sub-deacon responding:*

P. In nomine Patris, et Filii, et Spiritus Sancti. Amen.

In the name of the Father, and of the Son, and of the Holy Ghost. Amen.

P. Introibo ad altare Dei.

I will go in to the altar of God.

R. Ad Deum, qui lætificat juventutem meam.

To God, Who giveth joy to my youth.

P. Judica me, Deus, et discerne causam meam de gente non sancta: ab homine iniquo et doloso erue me.

Judge me, O God, and distinguish my cause from the nation that is not holy; deliver me from the unjust and deceitful man.

R. Quia tu es, Deus, fortitudo mea:

For Thou art, God, my strength; why

quare me repulisti, et quare tristis incedo, dum affligit me inimicus?

P. Emitte lucem tuam, et veritatem tuam: ipsa me deduxerunt, et adduxerunt in montem sanctum tuum, et in tabernacula tua.

R. Et introibo ad altare Dei: ad Deum, qui lætificat juventutem meam.

P. Confitebor tibi in cithara, Deus, Deus meus: quare tristis es anima mea, et quare conturbas me?

R. Spera in Deo, quoniam adhuc confitebor illi: salutare vultus mei, et Deus meus.

P. Gloria Patri, et Filio, et Spiritui sancto.

R. Sicut erat in principio, et nunc, et semper, et in sæcula sæculorum. Amen.

hast Thou cast me off and why do I go sorrowful whilst the enemy afflicteth me?

Send forth Thy light and Thy truth: they have conducted me, and brought me unto Thy holy hill, and into Thy tabernacles.

And I will go in to the altar of God; to God, Who giveth joy to my youth.

To Thee, O God, my God, I will give praise upon the harp: why art thou sad, O my soul, and why dost thou disquiet me?

Hope in God, for I will still give praise to Him, the salvation of my countenance and my God.

Glory be to the Father, and to the Son, and to the Holy Ghost.

As it was in the beginning, is now, and ever shall be, world without end. Amen.

P. Introibo ad altare Dei.

I will go in to the altar of God.

R. Ad Deum, qui lætificat juventutem meam.

To God, Who giveth joy to my youth.

Signing himself with the Sign of the Cross, he says:

P. Adjutorium nostrum in nomine Domini.

Our help is in the name of the Lord.

R. Qui fecit cœlum et terram.

Who made heaven and earth.

Bowing profoundly, the celebrant says:

P. Confiteor Deo omnipotenti, beatæ Mariæ semper virgini, beato Michaeli archangelo, beato Joanni Baptistæ, sanctis apostolis Petro et Paulo, omnibus sanctis, et vobis fratres, quia peccavi nimis cogitatione, verbo, et opere: mea culpa, mea culpa, mea maxima culpa. Ideo precor beatam Mariam semper virginem, beatum Michaelum archangelum, beatum Joannem Baptistam, sanctos apostolos Petrum et Paulum, omnes sanctos,

I confess to almighty God, to blessed Mary, ever virgin, to blessed Michael the archangel, to blessed John the Baptist, to the holy apostles Peter and Paul, to all the saints, and to you, brethren, that I have sinned exceedingly in thought, word, and deed; through my fault, through my fault, through my most grievous fault. Therefore I beseech the blessed Mary, ever virgin, blessed Michael the archangel, blessed John the

et vos fratres, orare pro me ad Dominum Deum nostrum.

R. Misereatur tui omnipotens Deus, et dimissis peccatis tuis, perducat te ad vitam æternam.

P. Amen.

R. Confiteor Deo omnipotenti, beatæ Mariæ semper virgini, beato Michaeli archangelo, beato Joanni Baptistæ, sanctis apostolis Petro et Paulo, omnibus sanctis, et tibi, Pater, quia peccavi nimis cogitatione, verbo, et opere: mea culpa, mea culpa, mea maxima culpa. Ideo precor beatam Mariam semper virginem, beatum Michaelem archangelum, beatum Joannem Baptistam, sanctos apostolos Petrum et Paulum, omnes sanctos, et te, Pater, orare pro

Baptist, the holy apostles Peter and Paul, all the saints, and you, brethren, to pray to the Lord our God for me.

May almighty God have mercy on you and, having forgiven you your sins, bring you to life everlasting.

Amen.

I confess to almighty God, to blessed Mary, ever virgin, to blessed Michael the archangel, to blessed John the Baptist, to the holy apostles Peter and Paul, to all the saints, and to you, Father, that I have sinned exceedingly in thought, word, and deed: through my fault, through my fault, through my most grievous fault. Therefore I beseech the blessed Mary, ever virgin, blessed Michael the archangel, blessed John the Baptist, the holy apos-

me ad Dominum Deum nostrum.

tles Peter and Paul, all the saints, and you, Father, to pray to the Lord our God for me.

P. Misereatur vestri omnipotens Deus, et dimissis peccatis vestris, perducat vos ad vitam æternam.

May almighty God have mercy on you and, having forgiven you your sins, bring you to life everlasting.

R. Amen.

Amen.

P. Indulgentiam, absolutionem, et remissionem peccatorum, nostrorum, tribuat nobis omnipotens et misericors Dominus.
R. Amen.

May the almighty and merciful God grant us pardon, absolution, and remission of our sins.

Amen.

Bowing, the celebrant continues:

P. Deus, tu conversus vivificabis nos.

Thou wilt turn again, O God, and quicken us.

R. Et plebs tua lætabitur in te.

And Thy people shall rejoice in Thee.

P. Ostende nobis, Domine, misericordiam tuam.

Show us, O Lord, Thy mercy.

R. Et salutare tuam da nobis.

And grant us Thy salvation.

P. Domine, exaudi orationem meam.

O Lord, hear my prayer.

R. Et clamor meus ad te veniat.

And let my cry come unto Thee.

P. Dominus vobiscum.

The Lord be with you.

R. Et cum spiritu tuo.

And with thy spirit.

P. Oremus.

Let us pray.

Ascending to the altar, the celebrant prays silently:

P. Aufer a nobis, quæsumus, Domine, iniquitates nostras: ut ad Sancta sanctorum puris mereamur mentibus introire. Per Christum Dominum nostrum.

Take away from us our iniquities, we beseech Thee, O Lord, that, being made pure in heart, we may be worthy to enter into the Holy of holies. Through Christ our Lord.

Amen.

Amen.

Kissing the altar where the relics of the saints repose, the celebrant says:

Oramus te, Domine, per merita sanctorum tuorum: quorum reliquiæ hic sunt, et omnium sanctorum: ut indulgere digneris omnia peccata mea. Amen.

We beseech Thee, O Lord, by the merits of those of Thy saints whose relics are here, and of all the saints, that Thou wouldst vouchsafe to pardon me all my sins. Amen.

At Solemn Mass, during the celebrant's preparatory prayer at the foot of the altar-steps, the choir sings the Introit and the Kyrie eleison before reading which himself, the celebrant blesses incense and casts it on the burning coals in the thurible, saying:

Ab illo benedicaris, in cujus honore cremaberis. Amen.

Mayest thou be blessed by Him in Whose honor thou art burnt. Amen.

Psalm LXXX. 17. Cibavit eos ex adipe frumenti: et et de petra, melle saturavit eos. Ps. ibid., 2. Exsultate Deo adjutori nostro; jubilate Deo Jacob. V. Gloria Patri et Filio et Spiritui Sancto; sicut erat in principio, et nunc, et semper, et in sæcula sæculorum. Amen.	Psalm LXXX. 17. He fed them with the fat of wheat; and filled them with honey out of the rock. Ps. ibid., 2. Rejoice to God our helper; sing aloud to the God of Jacob. V. Glory be to the Father, and to the Son, and to the Holy Ghost; as it was in the beginning, is now, and ever shall be; world without end. Amen.

Returning to the middle of the altar, the celebrant and ministers alternately pray:

P. Kyrie eleison.	Lord, mave mercy on us.
R. Kyrie eleison.	Lord, have mercy on us.
P. Kyrie eleison.	Lord, have mercy on us.
R. Christe eleison.	Christ, have mercy on us.
P. Christe eleison.	Christ, have mercy on us.
R. Christe eleison.	Christ, have mercy on us.
P. Kyrie eleison.	Lord, have mercy on us.

R. Kyrie eleison.　　Lord, have mercy on us.

P. Kyrie eleison.　　Lord, have mercy on us.

Stand *Standing at the of middle the altar, the celebrant intones the Gloria and continues its recital in a low tone.*

Sit *The Gloria is then taken up and sung by the choir during which the celebrant and his ministers sit until it is terminated.*

GLORIA in excelsis Deo, et in terra pax hominibus bonæ voluntatis. Laudamus te, benedicimus te, adoramus te, glorificamus te. Gratias agimus tibi propter magnam gloriam tuam. Domine Deus, Rex cœlestis, Deus Pater omnipotens. Domine Fili unigenite, Jesu Christe. Domine Deus, Agnus Dei, Filius Patris. Qui tollis peccata mundi, miserere nobis. Qui tollis peccata mundi, suscipe deprecationem nostram. Qui sedes ad dexteram Patris, miserere nobis. Quoniam tu solus sanctus. Tu solus Dominus. Tu solus

GLORY be to God on high, and on earth peace to men of good will. We praise Thee, we bless Thee, we adore Thee, we glorify Thee. We give Thee thanks for Thy great glory. O Lord God, heavenly king, God the Father almighty. O Lord Jesus Christ, the only begotten Son, O Lord God, Lamb of God, Son of the Father. Who takest away the sins of the world, have mercy on us. Who takest away the sins of the world, receive our prayer. Who sittest at the right hand of the Father, have mercy on us. For Thou alone art holy: Thou

altissimus, Jesu Christe, cum sancto Spiritu, in gloria Dei Patris. Amen.

alone art the Lord: Thou alone, O Jesus Christ, together with the Holy Ghost, art most high in the glory of God the Father. Amen.

Stand *The celebrant kisses the altar: then he turns to the people and salutes them, saying or singing:*

P. Dominus vobiscum.

R. Et cum spiritu tuo.

The Lord be with you,

And with thy spirit.

THE COLLECTS *Here follow the Collects which the celebrant, standing at the Missal, sings with hands uplifted.*

OREMUS: Deus, qui nobis sub Sacramento mirabili passionis tuae memoriam reliquisti; tribue quæsumus, ita nos corpo.is et sanguinis tui sacra mysteria venerari: ut redemptionis tuae fructum in nobis jugiter sentiamus: Qui vivis et regnas cum Deo Patre in unitate spiritus Sancti, Deus, per omnia sæcula sæculorum. Amen.

LET us pray: O God, Who under a wonderful Sacrament hast left us a memorial of Thy passion; grant us, we beseech Thee, so to venerate the sacred mysteries of Thy Body and Blood that we may evermore feel within us the fruit of Thy redemption: Who livest and reignest with God the Father in the unity of the Holy Ghost, God, world without end. Amen.

Sit

LECTIO Epistolae beati Pauli Apostoli ad Corinthios. I Cor. xi 23-29. Fratres: Ego enim accepi a Domino quod et tradidi vobis, quoniam Dominus Jesus in qua nocte tradebatur, accepit panem, et gratias agens fregit, et dixit: Accipite, et manducate: hoc est corpus meum, quod pro vobis tradetur: hoc facite in meam commemorationem. Similiter et calicem, postquam coenavit dicens: Hic calix novum testamentum est in meo sanguine. Hoc facite, quotiescumque bibetis, in meam commemorationem. Quotiescumque enim manducabitis panem hunc, et calicem bibetis, mortem Domini annuntiabitis, donec veniat. Itaque quicumque manduca-

THE Lesson is taken from the Epistle of Saint Paul to the Corinthians. I Cor. xi 23-29. Brethren: I have received of the Lord, that which also I have delivered to you, that the Lord Jesus, the same night in which He was betrayed, took bread, and giving thanks, broke, and said, Take ye, and eat: this is My body, which shall be delivered for you; this do for the commemoration of Me. In like manner also the chalice, after He had supped, saying, This chalice is the new testament in My blood; this do ye, as often as you shall drink, for the commemoration of Me. For as often as you shall eat this bread, and drink this chalice, you shall show

verit panem hunc, vel biberit calicem Domini indigne, reus erit corporis et sanguinis Domini. Probet autem seipsum homo: et sic de pane illo edat, et de calice bibat. Qui enim manducat et bibit indigne, judicium sibi manducat et bibit: non dijudicans corpus Domini.

the death of the Lord until he come. Therefore, whosoever shall eat this bread, or drink of the chalice of the Lord unworthily, shall be guilty of the body and of the blood of the Lord. But let a man prove himself: and so let him eat of that bread, and drink of the chalice. For

he that eateth and drinketh unworthily, eateth and drinketh judgment to himself, not discerning the body of the Lord.

R. Deo Gratias.   Thanks be to God.

THE GRADUAL   *The Gradual is the prayer following the Epistle said in a low tone by the celebrant.*

Psalm 144, 15-16. Oculi omnium in te sperant, Domine: et tu das illis escam in tempore opportuno. V. Aperis tu manum tuam: et imples omne animal benedictione. Alleluja, alleluja. V.

Ps. 144, 15-16. The eyes of all hope in Thee, O Lord, and Thou givest them meat in due season. V. Thou openest Thy hand, and fillest every living creature with Thy blessing. Alleluia, alleluia. V.

Joann. VI. 56-57. Caro mea vere est cibus, et sanguis meus vere est potus: Qui manducat meam

John VI. 56-57. My flesh is meat indeed, and My blood is drink indeed: he that eateth My flesh carnem, et bibit meum sanguinem, in me manet, et ego in eo. Alleluja.

and drinketh My blood, abideth in Me, and I in him. Alleluia.

After Septuagesima, instead of Alleluia and V, is said:

Tractus. Malach. I. 11. Ab ortu solis usque ad occasum, magnum est nomen meum in gentibus. V. Et in omni loco sacrificatur, et offertur nomini meo oblatio munda: quia magnum est nomen meum in gentibus. V. Prov. IX, 5. Venite, comedite panem meum; et bibete vinum, quod miscui vobis.

Tract. Mal. I. 11. From the rising of the sun even to the going down, My name is great among the gentiles. V. And in every place there is sacrifice, and there is offered to My name a clean offering: for My name is great among the gentiles. V. Prov. IX, 5. Come, eat My bread and drink the wine which I have mingled for you.

During the Octave of Corpus Christi, the Lauda Sion is said after the Gradual.

LAUDA SION

SION, lift thy voice and sing,
Praise thy Saviour and thy King,
Praise with hymns thy shepherd true.
Strive thy best to praise him well;
Yet doth he thy praise excel,
Never canst thou reach his due.

See today before us laid
Living and life-giving bread,

Theme for praise and joy profound.
Bread which at the sacred board
Was, by our Incarnate Lord,
Given to His Apostles round.

Let the praise be loud and high;
Full and tranquil be the joy
Felt today in every breast
On this festival divine,
Which records the origin
Of the glorious Eucharist.

On this table of the King,
Our new paschal offering
Brings to the end the olden rite;
Here, for empty shadows fled,
Is reality instead:
Here, instead of darkness, light.

His own act at supper seated,
Christ ordained to be repeated,
In his memory divine:
Wherefore now, with adoration,
We the Host of our salvation
Consecrate from bread and wine.

Hear what holy Church maintaineth
That the bread its substance changeth
Into Flesh, the wine to Blood.
Doth it pass thy comprehending?
Faith, the law of sight transcending,
Leaps to things not understood.

Here beneath these signs are hidden
Priceless things, to sense forbidden,
Signs, not things, are all we see.

Flesh from bread, and Blood from wine,
Yet is Christ in either sign,
All entire, confessed to be.

They too who of him partake,
Sever not, nor rend, nor break,
But entire their Lord receive.
Whether one or thousands eat,
All receive the selfsame meat,
Nor the less for others leave.

Both the wicked and the good
Eat of this celestial food;
But with ends how opposite!
Here 'tis life, and there 'tis death.
The same, yet issuing to each
In a difference infinite.

Nor a single doubt retain,
When they break the host in twain
But that in each part remains,
What was in the whole before;
Since the simple sign alone
Suffers change in state or form,
The signified remaining one
And the same for evermore.

Lo! upon the altar lies,
Hidden deep from human eyes,
Bread of angels from the skies,
Made the food of mortal man,
Children's meat, to dogs denied,
In old types foresignified;
In the manna heaven-supplied,
Isaac and the Paschal Lamb.

Jesu! Shepherd of the sheep,
Thou Thy flock in safety keep.

Living Bread! thy life supply;
Strengthen us or else we die;
Fill us with celestial grace:
Thou, who feedest us below!
Source of all we have or know!
Grant that with thy saints above,
Sitting at the feast of love,
We may see thee face to face.

Amen. Alleluia.

At Eastertide, instead of the Gradual, is said:

Alleluja, alleluja. V. Luc. XXIV. 35. Cognoverunt discipuli Dominum Jesum in fractione panis. Alleluja. V. Joann. VI. 56-57. Caro mea vere est cibus, et sanguis meus vere est potus: qui manducat meam carnem et bibit meum sanguinem, in me manet, et ego in eo. Alleluja.

Alleluia, alleluia. V. Luke XXIV. 35. The disciples knew the Lord Jesus in the breaking of the bread. Alleluia. V. John VI. 56-57. My flesh is meat indeed, and My blood is drink indeed: he that eateth My flesh and drinketh My blood abideth in Me and I in him. Alleluia.

The book is removed by the subdeacon to the Gospel side of the altar. While this is being done the celebrant bows down and says the "Munda cor meum." The people remain seated.

Munda cor meum, ac labia mea, omnipotens Deus, qui labia Isaiae prophetæ calculo mundasti ignito: ita me tua

Cleanse my heart and my lips, O almighty God, Who didst cleanse with a burning coal the lips of the prophet Isaias,

grata miseratione dignare mundare, ut sanctum Evangelium tuum digne valeam nuntiare. Per Christum Dominum nostrum. Amen.

Jube, Domine, benedicere.

Dominus sit in corde meo, et in labiis meis; ut digne et competenter annuntiem Evangelium suum. Amen.

and vouchsafe in Thy loving kindness so to purify me that I may be enabled worthily to announce Thy holy Gospel.

Through Christ our Lord. Amen.

Vouchsafe, O Lord, to bless me.

The Lord be in my heart and on my lips that I may worthily and becomingly announce His Gospel. Amen.

THE GOSPEL *Then going to the book at the Gospel side of the altar, the celebrant reads the Gospel in a low tone, beginning in this wise:*

Sit

P. Dominus vobiscum.

R. Et cum spiritu tuo.

P. Sequentia sancti Evangelii secundum Joannem.

R. Gloria tibi, Domine.

Joann. vi 56-59. In illo tempore; Dixit Jesus turbis Judaeorum: Caro mea vere est cibus, et sanguis meus vere est potus.

The Lord be with you.

And with thy spirit.

The continuation of the holy Gospel according to Saint John.

Glory be to Thee, O Lord.

John vi. 56-59. At that time: Jesus said to the multitudes of the Jews; My flesh is meat indeed, and My blood is drink indeed.

Qui manducat meam carnem, et bibit meum sanguinem, in me manet, et ego in illo. Sicut misit me vivens Pater, et ego vivo propter Patrem; et qui manducat me, et ipse vivet propter me. Hic est panis, qui de caelo descendit. Non sicut manducaverunt patres vestri manna, et mortui sunt. Qui manducat hunc panem, vivet in aeternum.

R. L a u s t i b i , Christi.

He that eateth My flesh, and drinketh My blood, abideth in me, and I in him. As the living Father hath sent Me, and I live by the Father, so he that eateth Me, the same also shall live by Me. This is the bread that came down from heaven. Not as your fathers did eat manna and are dead. He that eateth this bread shall live for ever.

Praise be to Thee, O Christ.

At solemn Mass, after the celebrant has completed the reading of the Gospel in a low tone of voice, he puts incense into the censer and blesses it. Then the deacon, kneeling on the altar-step, repeats the prayer "Munda cor meum" as above, and, taking the book of the holy Gospels from the altar, he kneels before the celebrant and asks his blessing:

Jube, domne, benedicere.

Pray, my Lord, a blessing.

The celebrant, blessing him, responds:

Dominus sit in corde tuo, et in labiis tuis: ut digne et competenter annunties E v a n g e l i u m suum: In nomine Patris, et Filii, et Spiritus Sancti. Amen.

The Lord be in thy heart and on thy lips, that thou mayest worthily and becomingly announce His Gospel. In the name of the Father, and of the Son, and of the Holy Ghost. Amen.

Stand *Then, accompanied by the other ministers with lights and incense, the deacon goes to the place appointed on the Gospel side in the sanctuary, sings the customary salutation, "Dominus vobis-um," announces the Gospel, signs the book and himself with the Sign of the Cross, incenses the book and proceeds to sing the Gospel as given before. During this time, the celebrant stands with hands joined facing the place where the deacon is singing the Gospel. At the end of the Gospel the subdeacon carries the book to the celebrant at the altar, who kisses it and says the prayer:*

Per evangelica dicta deleantur nostra delicta.

May our sins be blotted out by the words of the Holy Gospel.

Then the deacon incenses the celebrant.

THE CREDO *After the Gospel, the celebrant, standing at the mid-*
Stand *dle of the altar, intones the Credo and continues its recital in a low tone.*

Sit The Credo is then taken up and sung by the choir during which the celebrant and his ministers sit until it is terminated.

CREDO in unum Deum. Patrem omnipotentem, factorem cœli et terræ, visibilium omnium, et invisibilium. Et in unum Dominum Jesum Christum, Filium Dei unigenitum. Et ex Patre natum ante omnia sæcula. Deum de Deo, lumen de lumine, Deum verum de Deo vero. Genitum, non factum, consubstantialem Patri: per

I BELIEVE in one God. The Father almighty, maker of heaven and earth, and of all things visible and invisible. And in one Lord (*bow*), Jesus Christ, the only - begotten Son of God. Born of the Father before all ages. God of God, light of light, true God of true God. Begotten, not made; consubstantial with the Father; by Whom

quem omnia facta sunt. Qui propter nos homines, et propter nostram salutem descendit de cœlis. **_Kneel_** ET INCARNATUS EST DE SPIRITU SANCTO EX MARIA VIRGINE: ET HOMO FACTUS EST. **_Sit_** Crucifixus etiam pro nobis: sub Pontio Pilato passus, et sepultus est. Et resurrexit tertia die, secundum Scripturas. Et ascendit in cœlum; sedet ad dexteram Patris. Et iterum venturus est cum gloria judicare vivos, et mortuos: cujus regni non erit finis. Et in Spiritum Sanctum, Dominum, et vivificantem; qui ex Patre, Filioque procedit. Qui cum Patre et Filio simul adoratur et conglorificatur; qui locutus est per Prophetas. Et unam, sanctam, catholicam, et apostolicam Ecclesiam. Confiteor unum baptisma in remissionem peccatorum.

all things were made. Who for us men, and for our salvation came down from heaven. AND WAS MADE FLESH BY THE HOLY GHOST, OF THE VIRGIN MARY; AND WAS MADE MAN. He was crucified also for us, suffered under Pontius Pilate, and was buried. And the third day He rose again according to the Scriptures. And ascended into heaven. He sitteth at the right hand of the Father. And He shall come again with glory, to judge the living and the dead: and His kingdom shall have no end. And in the Holy Ghost, the Lord and Giver of life, Who proceedeth from the Father and the Son. Who, together with the Father and the Son, (*bow*) is adored and glorified; Who spoke by the prophets. And in one, holy, Catholic, and

Et exspecto resurrectionem mortuorum. Et vitam venturi sæculi. Amen. the resurrection of the dead. Of the world to come. Amen.

apostolic Church. I confess one Baptism for the remission of sins. And I expect the resurrection of the dead. And the life ✠ Amen.

In solemn Mass, shortly before the end of the Credo, the deacon rises and bowing to the celebrant carries the burse containing the corporal to the altar and spreads the corporal before the tabernacle. He then returns to his seat.

At the end of the Credo the celebrant proceeds to the Offertory. He kisses the altar; then turning to the people, he salutes them singing

P. Dominus vobiscum.

The Lord be with you.

R. Et cum spiritu tuo.

And with thy spirit.

Then, turning again to the altar, he continues:

P. Oremus.

Let us pray.

He then reads the Psalm-verse appointed.

THE OFFERTORY

Sit Levit. xxi 6. Sacerdotes Domini incensum et panes offerunt Deo: et ideo sancti erunt Deo suo, et non polluent nomen ejus.

Lev. xxi 6. The priests of the Lord offer incense and loaves to God, and therefore they shall be holy to their God, and shall not defile His name.

The celebrant then takes the paten on which rest two hosts, one for the priest's communion, the other for the exposition, and makes the oblation, saying: (In solemn Mass, while the preceding prayer is being read, the subdeacon, with the humeral veil about his shoulders, carries the chalice with its appurtenances from the credence table to the altar.)

SUSCIPE, sancte Pater, omnipotens æterne Deus, hanc immaculatam hostiam, quam ego dignus famulus tuus offero tibi, Deo meo vivo et vero, pro innumerabilibus peccatis, et offensionibus et negligentiis meis, et pro omnibus circumstantibus, sed et pro omnibus fidelibus christianis vivis atque defunctis: ut mihi, et illis proficiat ad salutem in vitam æternam. Amen.

RECEIVE, O holy Father, almighty and eternal God, this spotless host, which I, Thy unworthy servant, offer unto Thee, my living and true God, for my countless sins, trespasses and omissions, likewise for all here present; and for all faithful Christians, whether living or dead, that it may avail both me and them to salvation unto life everlasting. Amen.

The celebrant makes the Sign of the Cross with the paten and places the hosts upon the corporal. He then pours wine and water into the chalice (in solemn Mass the deacon serves the wine—the subdeacon the water) and recites the prayer:

Deus, qui humanæ substantiæ dignitatem mirabiliter condidisti, et mirabilius reformasti: da nobis per hujus aquæ et vini mysterium, ejus divinitatis esse consortes, qui humanitatis nostræ fieri dignatus est particeps, Jesus Christus Filius tuus Dominus nos-

O God, Who in creating man didst exalt His nature very wonderfully and yet more wonderfully didst establish it anew: by the mystery signified in the mingling of this water and wine grant us to have part in the Godhead of Him Who hath vouchsafed to

ter: Qui tecum vivit et regnat in unitate Spiritus sancti, Deus; per omnia sæcula sæculorum. Amen.

share our manhood, Jesus Christ Thy Son, Our Lord, Who liveth and reigneth with Thee in the unity of the Holy Ghost, God, world without end. Amen.

The celebrant then offers the chalice with the words:

Offerimus tibi, Domine, calicem salutaris, tuam deprecantes clementiam: ut in conspectu divinæ majestatis tuæ, pro nostra et totius mundi salute cum odore suavitatis ascendat. Amen.

We offer unto Thee, O Lord, the chalice of salvation, beseeching Thy clemency that it may ascend as a sweet odor before Thy divine majesty, for our own salvation, and for that of the whole world. Amen.

In solemn Mass the subdeacon receives the paten, covers it with the veil, and holding it thus, retires to the center of the altar at the foot of the steps where he remains until towards the end of the Pater Noster.

The celebrant forms the Sign of the Cross with the chalice, places it upon the corporal, covers it, bows and says:

In spiritu humilitatis, et in animo contrito, suscipiamur a te, Domine: et sic fiat sacrificium nostrum in conspectu tuo hodie, ut placeat tibi, Domine Deus.

Humbled in mind, and contrite of heart, may we find favor with Thee, O Lord: and may the sacrifice we this day offer up be well-pleasing to Thee, Who art our Lord and our God.

Veni, sanctificator, omnipotens æterne Deus, et benedic ✠ hoc sacrificium tuo sancto nomini præparatum.

Come, Thou, the sanctifier, God almighty and everlasting; bless ✠ this sacrifice which is prepared for the glory of Thy holy name.

In solemn Mass, incense is then blessed, the celebrant saying:

Per intercessionem beati Michaelis archangeli stantis a dexteris altaris incensi, et omnium electorum suorum, incensum istud dignetur Dominus benedicere, et in odorem suavitatis accipere. Per Christum Dominum nostrum. Amen.

By the intercession of blessed Michael the archangel, who standeth at the right hand of the altar of incense, and of all his elect, may the Lord vouchsafe to bless this incense, and to receive it for an odor of sweetness. Through Christ our Lord. Amen.

He incenses the bread and wine on the altar with the words:

In censum istud a te benedictum, ascendat ad te Domine, et descendat super nos misericordia tua.

May this incense, blessed by Thee, ascend before Thee, O Lord, and may Thy mercy descend upon us.

He then incenses the altar, saying:

Dirigatur, Domine, oratio mea, sicut incensum. in conspectu

Let my prayer be directed, O Lord, as incense, in Thy sight;

tuo; elevatio manuum mearum sacrificium vespertinum. Pone, Domine, custodiam ori meo, et ostium circumstantiæ labiis meis; ut non declinet cor meum in verba malitiæ, ad excusandas excusationes in peccatis.

the lifting up of my hands as an evening sacrifice. Set a watch, O Lord, before my mouth: and a door round about my lips: that my heart may not incline to evil words: to make excuses in sins.

The celebrant returns the thurible to the deacon, saying:

Accendat in nobis Dominus ignem sui amoris, et flammam æternæ caritatis. Amen.

May the Lord enkindle in us the fire of His love and the flame of everlasting charity. Amen.

Then the deacon incenses the celebrant, clergy and the subdeacon: after which he is himself incensed by the thurifer, who lastly incenses the laity.

Stand   *Lastly the people are incensed.*

Sit *After the offering of the chalice (in solemn Mass, after the incensation) the celebrant, standing at the Epistle side of the altar, washes his fingers, saying:*

Lavabo inter innocentesmanusmeas: et circumdabo altare tuum, Domine.

I will wash my hands among the innocent: and will compass Thine altar, O Lord.

Ut audiam vocem laudis: et enarrem universa mirabilia tua.

That I may hear the voice of praise: and tell of all Thy wondrous works.

Domine, dilexi decorem domus tuæ, et locum habitationis gloriæ tuæ.

Ne perdas cum impiis, Deus, animam meam: et cum viris sanguinum vitam meam.

In quorum manibus iniquitates sunt: dextera eorum repleta est muneribus.

Ego autem in innocentia mea ingressus sum: redime me, et miserere mei.

Pes meus stetit in directo: in ecclesiis benedicam te, Domine.

Gloria Patri, et Filio, et Spiritui sancto.

Sicut erat in principio, et nunc, et semper; et in sæcula sæculorum. Amen.

I have loved, O Lord, the beauty of Thy house, and the place where Thy glory dwelleth.

Take not away my soul, O God, with the wicked: nor my life with men of blood.

In whose hands are iniquities; their right hand is filled with gifts.

But as for me, I have walked in my innocence: redeem me, and have mercy on me.

My foot hath stood in the direct way: in the churches I will bless Thee, O Lord.

Glory be to the Father, and to the Son, and to the Holy Ghost.

As it was in the beginning, is now, and ever shall be: world without end. Amen.

The celebrant returns to the middle of the altar, bows and says:

Suscipe, sancta Trinitas, hanc oblationem, quam tibi

Receive, O holy Trinity, this oblation offered up by us

offerimus ob memoriam passionis, resurrectionis, et ascensionis Jesu Christi Domini nostri; et in honorem beatæ Mariæ semper virginis, et beati Joannis Baptistæ, et sanctorum apostolorum Petri et Pauli, et istorum, et omnium sanctorum: ut illis proficiat ad honorem, nobis autem ad salutem; et illi pro nobis intercedere dignentur in cœlis, quorum memoriam agimus in terris. Per eumdem Christum Dominum nostrum. Amen.

to Thee, in memory of the passion, resurrection, and ascension of Our Lord Jesus Christ, and in honor of blessed Mary, ever a virgin, of blessed John the Baptist, of the holy apostles Peter and Paul, of these, and of all of the saints, that it may be available to their honor and to our salvation: and may they whose memory we celebrate on earth vouchsafe to intercede for us in heaven. Through the same Christ our Lord. Amen.

THE "ORATE FRATRES" *Kissing the altar and turning to the people, the celebrant says:*

P. Orate, fratres, ut meum ac vestrum sacrificium acceptabile fiat apud Deum Patrem omnipotentem.

Brethren, pray that my sacrifice and yours may be well pleasing to God the Father almighty.

Suscipiat Dominus sacrificium de manibus tuis, ad laudem et gloriam nominis sui, ad utilitatem quoque nostram, to-

May the Lord receive this sacrifice at thy hands, to the praise and glory of His name, to our own benefit, and to that tiusque Ecclesiæ suæ sanctæ.

P. Amen (in a low voice.)

of all His holy Church. Amen.

THE SECRET *The celebrant then, in a low voice, reads the Secret*

Ecclesiae tuae, quaesumus, Domine, unitatis et pacis propitius dona concede; quae sub oblatis muneribus mystice designantur. Per Dominum nostrum Jesum Christum, Filium tuum, qui tecum vivit et regnat in unitate Spiritus Sancti, Deus, per omnia sæcula sæculorum. Amen.

In Thy mercy, O Lord, we beseech Thee, grant to Thy Church the gifts of unity and peace, which are mystically signified by the gifts which we offer up. Through our Lord Jesus Christ, Thy Son, Who liveth and reigneth with Thee in the unity of the Holy Ghost, God, world without end. Amen.

THE PREFACE *The celebrant then chants the Preface*

Stand

P. Dominus vobiscum.

R. Et cum spiritu tuo.

P. Sursum corda.

R. Habemus ad Dominum.

P. Gratias agamus Domino Deo nostro.

R. Dignum et justum est.

The Lord be with you.

And with thy spirit.

Lift up your hearts.

We have lifted them up unto the Lord.

Let us give thanks to the Lord our God.

It is meet and just.

P. Vere dignum et justum est, aequuam et salutare, nos tibi semper, et ubique gratias agere: Domine sancte, Pater omnipotens, æterne Deus, Quia per incarnati Verbi mysterium, nova mentis nostræ oculis tuæ claritatis infulsit: ut dum visibiliter Deum cognoscimus, per hunc in invisibilium amorem rapiamur. Et ideo cum angelis et archangelis, cum thronis et dominationibus, cumque omni militia cœlestis exercitus, hymnum gloriæ tuæ canimus, sine fine dicentes:

It is truly meet and just, right and profitable for us, at all times, and in all places, to give thanks to Thee, O Lord, the holy One, the Father almighty, the everlasting God: because by the Mystery of the Word made Flesh, from Thy brightness a new light hath risen to shine on the eyes of our souls, in order that, God becoming visible to us, we may be borne upward to the love of things invisible. And therefore, with the angels and archangels, with the thrones and dominations, and with all the array of the heavenly host we sing a hymn to Thy glory and unceasingly repeat:

The celebrant does not sing the following. It is sung by the choir.

Kneel Sanctus, sanctus, sanctus Dominus, Deus Sabaoth. Pleni sunt cæli et terra gloria tua. Hosanna in excelsis. Benedictus qui venit in

Holy, holy, holy Lord God of hosts. The heavens and the earth are full of Thy glory. Hosanna in the highest. Blessed is He that cometh in

nomine Domini. Hosanna in excelsis.

the name of the Lord. Hosanna in the highest.

At the Sanctus the bell is rung thrice. (When the Blessed Sacrament is exposed the bell is not rung.)

THE CANON *The celebrant raises his eyes and hands, then bows and says:*

Te igitur, clementissime Pater, per Jesum Christum Filium tuum, Dominum nostrum, supplices rogamus, ac petimus,

Wherefore, we humbly pray and beseech Thee, most merciful Father, through Jesus Christ, Thy Son, our Lord to

Here the celebrant kisses the altar.

uti accepta habeas, et benedicas, hæc ✠ dona, hæc ✠ munera, hæc ✠ sancta sacrificia illibata, in primis, quæ tibi offerimus pro Ecclesia tua sancta catholica : quam pacificare, custodire, adunare, et regere digneris toto orbe terrarum: una cum famulo tuo Papa nostro N. et Antistite nostro N. et omnibus orthodoxis, atque catholicæ, et apostolicæ fidei cultoribus.

receive and to bless these ✠ gifts, these ✠ presents, these ✠ holy unspotted sacrifices, which we offer up to Thee, in the first place, for Thy holy Catholic Church, that it may please Thee to grant her peace, to guard, unite, and guide her throughout the world; as also for Thy servant N., our Pope, and N., our bishop, and for all who are orthodox in belief and who profess the catholic and apostolic faith.

Commemoration of the Living

Memento, Domine, famulorum famularumque tuarum N. et N.

Be mindful, O Lord, of Thy servants N. and N.

The celebrant here names those for whom he wishes to pray especially.

Et omnium circumstantium, quorum tibi fides cognita est, et nota devotio, pro quibus tibi offerimus: vel qui tibi offerunt hoc sacrificium laudis, pro se, suisque omnibus: pro redemptione animarum suarum, pro spe salutis, et incolumitatis suæ: tibique reddunt vota sua æterno Deo, vivo et vero.

And of all here present, whose faith and devotion are known to Thee, for whom we offer, or who offer up to Thee, this sacrifice of praise, for themselves, their families, and their friends, for the salvation of their souls, and the health and welfare they hope for, and who now pay their vows to Thee, God eternal, living, and true.

Commemoration of the Saints

Communicantes, et memoriam venerantes, in primis gloriosæ semper virginis Mariæ, genitricis Dei et Domini nostri Jesu Christi; sed et beatorum apostolorum ac martyrum tu-

Having communion with and venerating the memory, first, of the glorious Mary, ever a virgin, Mother of Jesus Christ, our God and our Lord; likewise of Thy blessed apostles

orum Petri et Pauli, Andreæ Jacobi, Joannis, Thomæ, Jacobi, Philippi, Bartholomæi, Matthæi, Simonis et Thaddæi; Lini, Cleti, Clementis, Xysti, Cornelii, Cypriani, Laurentii, Chrysogoni, Joannis et Pauli, Cosmæ et Damiani: et omnium sanctorum tuorum; quorum meritis precibusque concedas, ut in omnibus protectionis tuæ muniamur auxilio. Per eumdem Christum Dominum nostrum. Amen.

and martyrs, Peter and Paul, Andrew, James, John, Thomas, James, Philip, Bartholomew, Matthew, Simon, and Thaddaeus; of Linus, Cletus, Clement, Xystus, Cornelius, Cyprian, Lawrence, Chrysogonus, John and Paul, Cosmas and Damian, and of all Thy saints: for the sake of whose merits and prayers do Thou grant that in all things we may be defended by the help of Thy protection. Through the same Christ our Lord. Amen.

Spreading his hands over the chalice, the celebrant says:
(The bell is here rung to announce that the Consecration is about to take place.) (When the Blessed Sacrament is exposed the bell is not rung.)

Hanc igitur oblationem servitutis nostræ, sed et cunctæ familiæ tuæ, quæsumus, Domine, ut placatus accipias: diesque nostros in tua pace disponas, atque ab æterna damnatione nos eripi, et

Wherefore, we beseech Thee, O Lord, graciously to receive this oblation which we, Thy servants, and with us Thy whole family, offer up to Thee: dispose our days in Thy peace; command that

THE CONSECRATION OF THE HOST.
"HOC EST ENIM CORPUS MEUM."
"THIS IS MY BODY"

THE ELEVATION OF THE HOST.
"MY LORD AND MY GOD."

in electorum tuorum jubeas grege numerari. Per Christum Dominum nostrum. Amen.

we be saved from eternal damnation and numbered among the flock of Thine elect. Through Christ our Lord. Amen.

(The celebrant makes the Sign of the Cross thrice over the bread and wine; then once over the host and once over the chalice.)

Quam oblationem tu, Deus, in omnibus, quæsumus, bene ✠ dictam, adscrip ✠ tam, ra ✠ tam, rationabilem, acceptabilemque, facere digneris: ut nobis cor ✠ pus et san ✠ guis fiat dilectissimi Filii tui Domini nostri Jesu Christi.

And do Thou, O God, vouchsafe in all respects to bless, ✠ consecrate, ✠ and approve ✠ this our oblation, to perfect it and to render it well-pleasing to Thyself, so that it may become for us the body ✠ and blood ✠ of Thy most beloved Son, Jesus Christ our Lord.

The celebrant continues:

Qui pridie quam pateretur, accepit panem in sanctas, ac venerabiles manus suas; et elevatis oculis in cœlum ad te Deum Patrem suum omnipotentem, tibi gratias agens, bene ✠ dixit, fregit, deditque discipulis suis,

Who the day before He suffered, took bread into His holy and venerable hands, and having lifted up His eyes to heaven, to Thee, God, His almighty Father, giving thanks to Thee, blessed it ✠, broke it, and gave it to His

dicens: Accipite. et manducate ex hoc omnes.

disciples, saying: Take ye and eat ye all of this.

The Consecration and Elevation of the Host

HOC EST ENIM COR-PUS MEUM.

FOR THIS IS MY BODY.*

The celebrant genuflects, e'evates the Host. and genuflects again. (The bell is rung three times.) (When the Blessed Sacrament is exposed the bell is not rung.)

. Uncovering the chalice the celebrant proceeds:

Simili modo postquam cœnatum est. accipiens et hunc præclarum calicem in sanctas, ac venerabiles manus suas: item tibi gratias agens, bene✠dixit, deditque dicipulis suis, dicens: Accipite, et bibite ex eo omnes;

In like manner. after He had supped. taking into His holy and venerable hands this goodly chalice. again giving thanks to Thee, He blessed ✠ it, and gave it to His disciples, saying: Take ye, and drink ye all of this: FOR

The Consecration of the Wine. The Elevation of the Chalice

HIC EST ENIM CALIX SANGUINIS MEI. NOVI ET ÆTERNI TESTAMENTI: MYS-TERIUM FIDEI: QUI

THIS IS THE CHALICE OF MY BLOOD, OF THE NEW AND EVERLAST-ING TESTAMENT: THE MYSTERY OF FAITH:

*(Pope Pius X, on May 18, 1907, granted an indulgence of seven years and seven quarantines, to all the faithful, who, at the Elevation during Mass, or at public exposition of the Blessed Sacrament, look at the sacred host and devoutly say: "My Lord and my God!")

THE CONSECRATION OF THE WINE.
"HIC EST ENIM CALIX SANGUINIS MEI."
"FOR THIS IS MY BLOOD."

THE ELEVATION OF THE CHALICE.

"Which shall be shed for many unto remission of sins."   Matth. xxvi, 28.

PRO VOBIS ET PRO MULTIS EFFUNDETUR IN REMISSIONEM PECCATORUM. Hæc quotiescumque feceritis, in mei memoriam facietis.

WHICH FOR YOU AND FOR MANY SHALL BE SHED UNTO THE REMISSION OF SINS. As often as ye shall do these things, ye shall do them in memory of Me.

The celebrant genuflects, elevates the chalice, genuflects again (the bell is rung three times) (when the Blessed Sacrament is exposed the bell is not rung) and, covering the chalice, continues:

Unde et memores, Domine, nos servi tui, sed et plebs tua sancta, ejusdem Christi Filii tui Domini nostri tam beatæ passionis, nec non et ab inferis resurrectionis, sed et in cœlos gloriosæ ascensionis: offerimus præclaræ majestati tuæ de tuis donis, ac datis, hostiam✠ puram, hostiam ✠

Wherefore, O Lord, we, Thy servants, as also Thy holy people, calling to mind the blessed passion of the same Christ, Thy Son, our Lord, His resurrection from the grave, and His glorious ascension into heaven, offer up to Thy most excellent majesty of Thine own gifts bestowed upon us, a victim ✠ which is pure, a

The celebrant makes the Sign of the Cross three times over the Host and chalice together; then once over the Host and once over the chalice.

sanctam, hostiam ✠ immaculatam, panem ✠ sanctum vitæ æternæ, et calicem ✠ salutis perpetuæ.

victim ✠ which is holy, ✠ a victim ✠ which is stainless, the holy bread ✠ of life everlasting, and the chalice ✠ of eternal salvation.

Supra quæ propitio ac sereno vultu respicere digneris: et accepta habere, sicuti accepta habere dignatus es munera pueri tui justi Abel, et sacrificium Patriarchæ nostri Abrahæ: et quod tibi obtulit summus sacerdos tuus Melchisedech, sanctum sacrificium, immaculatam hostiam.

Vouchsafe to look upon them with a gracious and tranquil countenance, and to accept them, even as Thou wast pleased to accept the offerings of Thy just servant, Abel, and the sacrifice of Abraham, our patriarch, and that which Melchisedech, Thy high priest, offered up to Thee, a holy sacrifice, a victim without blemish.

The celebrant bows and prays:

Supplices te rogamus omnipotens Deus, jube hæc perferri per manus sancti angeli tui in sublime altare tuum, in conspectu divinæ majestatis tuæ, ut quotquot ex hac altaris

We humbly beseech Thee, almighty God, to command that these our offerings be borne by the hands of Thy holy angel, to Thine altar on high, in the presence of Thy divine majesty, that as

Here the celebrant kisses the altar:

participatione sacrosanctum Filii tui Cor✠pus et San✠guinem sumpserimus,

many of us as shall receive the most sacred ✠ body and ✠ blood of Thy Son by

omni benedictione cœlesti et gratia repleamur. Per eumdem Christum Dominum nostrum. Amen.

partaking thereof from this altar may be filled with every heavenly blessing and grace. Through the same Christ our Lord. Amen.

The Commemoration of the Dead

Memento etiam, Domine, famulorum famularumque tuarum N. et N. qui nos præcesserunt cum signo fidei, et dormiunt in somno pacis.

Be mindful, also, O Lord, of Thy servants, N. and N., who have gone before us with the sign of faith and who sleep the sleep of peace.

The celebrant mentions those for whom he wishes to pray especially.

Ipsis, Domine, et omnibus in Christo quiescentibus, locum refrigerii, lucis et pacis, ut indulgeas, deprecamur. Per eumdem Christum Dominum nostrum. Amen.

To these, O Lord, and to all who rest in Christ, grant, we beseech Thee, a place of refreshment, light, and peace. Through the same Christ our Lord. Amen.

Striking his breast, the celebrant says:

Nobis quoque peccatoribus famulis tuis, de multitudine miserationum tuarum sperantibus, partem aliquam, et societa-

To us sinners, also Thy servants, who put our trust in the multitude of Thy mercies, vouchsafe to grant some part and

tem donare digneris, cum tuis sanctis apostolis et martyribus; cum Joanne, Stephano, Matthia, Barnaba, Ignatio, Alexandro, Marcellino, Petro, Felicitate, Perpetua, Agatha, Lucia, Agnete, Cæcilia, Anastasia, et omnibus sanctis tuis: intra quorum nos consortium, non æstimator meriti, sed veniæ, quæsumus, largitor admitte. Per Christum Dominum nostrum.

fellowship with Thy holy apostles and martyrs: with John, Stephen, Matthias, Barnabas, Ignatius, Alexander, Marcellinus, Peter, Felicitas, Perpetua, Agatha, Lucy, Agnes, Cecilia, Anastasia, and with all Thy saints. Into their company do Thou, we beseech Thee, admit us, not weighing our merits, but freely pardoning our offenses. Through Christ our Lord.

The celebrant makes the Sign of the Cross three times over the Host and chalice, saying:

Per quem hæc omnia, Domine, semper bona creas, sancti✠ficas, vivi ✠ficas, bene✠dicis et præstas nobis.

By whom, O Lord, Thou dost always create, sanctify, ✠ quicken, ✠ bless, ✠ and bestow upon us all these good things.

The celebrant uncovers the chalice, genuflects, makes the Sign of the Cross with the Host thrice over the chalice and twice between the chalice and himself, and elevates both slightly, saying the while:

Per ip✠sum, et cum ip✠so, et in ip✠so, est tibi Deo Patri ✠ omnipotenti, in unitate Spiritus ✠

Through Him, ✠ and with Him, ✠ and in Him, ✠ is to Thee, ✠ God the Father ✠ almighty,

sancti, omnis honor, et gloria.

in the unity of the Holy ✠ Ghost, all honor and glory.

The celebrant now sings the Pater Noster.

P. Per omnia sæcula sæculorum.

World without end.

R. Amen.

Amen.

P. Oremus. Præceptis salutaribus, moniti, et divina institutione formati, audemus dicere;

Let us pray. Admonished by salutary precepts, and following divine directions, we presume to say:

Pater noster, qui es in cœlis; Sanctificetur nomen tuum: Adveniat regnum tuum: Fiat voluntas tua, sicut in cœlo, et in terra. Panem nostrum quotidianum da nobis hodie: Et dimitte nobis debita nostra, sicut et nos dimittimus debitoribus nostris. Et ne nos inducas in tentationem.

Our Father, Who art in heaven, hallowed be Thy name: Thy kingdom come: Thy will be done on earth as it is in heaven. Give us this day our daily bread; and forgive us our trespasses as we forgive those who trespass against us. And lead us not into temptation.

R. Sed libera nos a malo.

But deliver us from evil.

P. Amen (in a low voice.)

Amen.

At solemn Mass, the deacon, towards the end of the Pater Noster, goes to the right hand of the celebrant, where he awaits the approach of the subdeacon, from whom he receives the paten, which he puts into the hands of the celebrant.
Holding the paten, the celebrant says:

Libera nos, quæsumus, Domine, ab omnibus malis, præteritis, præsentibus, et futuris; et intercedente beata, et gloriosa semper virgine Dei genitrice Maria, cum beatis apostolis tuis Petro et Paulo, atque Andrea, et omnibus sanctis,

Deliver us, we beseech Thee, O Lord, from all evils, past, present, and to come; and by the intercession of the blessed and glorious Mary, ever a virgin, mother of God, and of Thy holy apostles Peter and Paul, of Andrew, and of all the saints,

Making the Sign of the Cross with the paten and kissing it, the celebrant continues:

Da propitius pacem in diebus nostris: ut ope misericordiæ tuæ adjuti, et a peccato simus semper liberi, et ab omni perturbatione securi.

Graciously grant peace in our days, that through the help of Thy bountiful mercy we may always be free from sin, and secure from all disturbance.

The celebrant uncovers the chalice, genuflects, breaks the Host into two parts, saying:

Per eumdem Dominum nostrum Jesum Christum Filium tuum.

Through the same Jesus Christ, Thy Son, our Lord.

Breaking a particle from the portion in his left hand, the celebrant says:

Qui tecum vivit et regnat in unitate Spiritus sancti Deus,

Who liveth and reigneth with Thee in the unity of the Holy Ghost, God,

P. Per omnia sæcula sæculorum.

R. Amen.

World without end. Amen.

With the particle he makes the Sign of the Cross three times over the chalice, saying:

P. Pax ✠ Domini sit ✠ semper vobis- ✠ cum.

R. Et cum spiritu tuo.

May the peace ✠ of the Lord be ✠ always with ✠ you.

And with thy spirit.

He drops the particle into the chalice, saying:

Hæc commixtio et consecratio, Corporis et Sanguinis Domini nostri Jesu Christi, fiat accipientibus nobis in vitam æternam. Amen.

May this commingling and consecrating of the body and blood of our Lord Jesus Christ avail us who receive it unto life everlasting. Amen.

The celebrant covers the chalice, genuflects, bows, and strikes his breast three times, saying:

Agnus Dei, qui tollis peccata mundi, miserere nobis.

Lamb of God, Who takest away the sins of the world,
Have mercy on us.

Agnus Dei, qui tollis peccata mundi, miserere nobis.

Lamb of God, Who takest away the sins of the world,
Have mercy on us.

Agnus Dei, qui tollis peccata mundi, dona nobis pacem.

Lamb of God, Who takest away the sins of the world,
Grant us peace.

Bowing, the celebrant says:

Domine Jesu Christe, qui dixisti apostolis tuis; pacem relinquo vobis, pacem meam do vobis: ne respicias peccata mea, sed fidem Ecclesiæ tuæ: eamque secundum voluntatem tuam pacificare et coadunare digneris: qui vivis et regnas Deus, per omnia sæcula sæculorum. Amen.

O Lord Jesus Christ, Who didst say to Thine apostles: Peace I leave you, My peace I give you; look not upon my sins but upon the faith of Thy Church: and vouchsafe to grant her peace and unity according to Thy will, Who livest and reignest, God, world without end. Amen.

At solemn Mass the deacon is saluted by the celebrant with the "Kiss of Peace" with these words:

P. Pax tecum.

Peace be with thee.

The deacon answers:

R. Et cum spiritu tuo.

And with thy spirit.

The deacon then salutes in like manner the subdeacon, who in turn salutes the clergy who may be assisting at the Mass. The celebrant continues:

Domine Jesu Christe, Fili Dei vivi, qui ex voluntate Patris, cooperante Spiritu sancto, per mortem tuam mundum vivificasti: libera me per hoc sacrosanctum Corpus et Sanguinem tuum

Lord Jesus Christ, Son of the living God, Who, according to the will of the Father, through the co-operation of the Holy Ghost, hast by Thy death given life to the world; deliver me by this Thy most

ab omnibus iniquitatibus meis, et universis malis: et fac me tuis semper inhærere mandatis, et a te nunquam separari permittas: qui cum eodem Deo Patre et Spiritu sancto vivis et regnas Deus in sæcula sæculorum.

Amen.

Perceptio corporis tui, Domine Jesu Christe, quod ego indignus sumere præsumo, non mihi proveniat in judicium et condemnationem: sed pro tua pietate prosit mihi ad tutamentum mentis et corporis, et ad medelam percipiendam: qui vivis et regnas cum Deo Patre in unitate Spiritus sancti Deus, per omnia sæcula sæculorum.
Amen.

sacred body, and blood from all my iniquities, and from every evil. Make me always cleave to Thy commandments and never suffer me to be separated from Thee: Who with the same God the Father and the Holy Ghost livest and reignest, God, world without end.
Amen.

Let not the partaking of Thy body, O Lord Jesus Christ, which I, all unworthy, presume to receive, turn to my judgment and condemnation; but through Thy loving kindness may it be to me a safeguard and remedy for soul and body; Who, with God the Father, in the unity of the Holy Ghost, livest and reignest, God, world without end.
Amen.

The priest genuflects and says:

Panem coelestem

I will take the

accipiam et nomen Domini invocabo.

bread of heaven and will call upon the name of the Lord.

Bowing and striking his breast, the celebrant says three times:

Domine, non sum dignus, ut intres sub tectum meum; sed tantum dic verbo, et sanabitur anima mea.

Lord, I am not worthy that Thou shouldst enter under my roof: but only say the word and my soul shall be healed.

(*The bell is rung to announce the time of Communion*)
(*When the Blessed Sacrament is exposed the bell is not rung*)
Holding the Host in his right hand, the celebrant says:

Corpus Domini nostri Jesu Christi custodiat animam meam in vitam æternam. Amen.

May the body of Our Lord Jesus Christ keep my soul unto life everlasting. Amen.

The celebrant, after making the Sign of the Cross with the Host receives it and pauses for a moment's communion with his God, then, uncovering the chalice, he genuflects, gathers any fragments from the corporal and puts them into the chalice, saying meanwhile:

Quid retribuam Domino pro omnibus, quæ retribuit mihi? Calicem salutaris accipiam, et nomen Domini invocabo. Laudans invocabo Dominum, et ab inimicis meis salvus ero.

What shall I render unto the Lord for all the things that He hath rendered unto me? I will take the chalice of salvation and will call upon the name of the Lord. With high praises will I call upon the Lord, and I shall be saved from all mine enemies.

**THE EXPOSITION OF THE BLESSED SACRA-
MENT DURING THE MASS ON THE FIRST DAY**

Sanguis Domini nostri Jesu Christi custodiat animam meam in vitam æternam. Amen.

May the blood of Our Lord Jesus Christ keep my soul unto life everlasting. Amen.

The celebrant receives the Precious Blood and pauses for a moment's thanksgiving.

Having consumed the Precious Blood, the celebrant, with the aid of the deacon, if the Mass be solemn, places the second consecrated Host in the ostensorium which stands on the corporal in front of the tabernacle. He then genuflects in adoration and proceeds with the Mass.

During the rest of the Mass the celebrant genuflects before the Blessed Sacrament exposed, when passing to or from the center of the altar, as also before and after turning towards the people.

COMMUNION OF THE FAITHFUL *When the priest receives the Precious Blood, the Confiteor is said. (Unless necessity demands, Holy Communion is not distributed from the altar on which the Blessed Sacrament is exposed; but from a side altar.)*

R. Confiteor Deo omnipotenti, beatæ Mariæ semper virgini, beato Michaeli archangelo, beato Joanni Baptistæ, sanctis apostolis Petro et Paulo, omnibus sanctis, et tibi, pater, quia peccavi nimis cogitatione, verbo, et opere: mea culpa, mea culpa, mea maxima culpa. Ideo precor beatam Mariam semper virginem, beatum Michaelem

I confess to almighty God, to blessed Mary, ever virgin, to blessed Michael the archangel, to blessed John the Baptist, to the holy apostles Peter and Paul, to all the saints, and to you, Father, that I have sinned exceedingly in thought, word, and deed: through my fault, through my fault, through my most grievous fault.

archangelum, beatum Joannem Baptistam, sanctos apostolos Petrum et Paulum, omnes sanctos et te, pater, orare pro me ad Dominum Deum nostrum.

Therefore I beseech the blessed Mary, ever virgin, blessed Michael the archangel, blessed John the Baptist, the holy apostles, Peter and Paul and all the saints, and you Father, to pray to the Lord Our God, for me.

The celebrant genuflects, turns to the people and says:

P. Misereatur vestri omnipotens Deus, et dimissis peccatis vestris, perducat vos ad vitam æternam.
R. Amen.
P. Indulgentiam, ✠ absolutionem, et remissionem peccatorum vestrorum, tribuat vobis omnipotens et misericors Dominus.
R. Amen.

May almighty God have mercy on you, and, having forgiven you your sins, bring you to life everlasting. Amen.
May the almighty and merciful Lord grant you pardon, absolution, ✠ and remission of your sins. Amen.

Facing the communicants and holding a Sacred Particle in his hand. the celebrant says:

P. Ecce Agnus Dei, ecce qui tollit peccata mundi:

Behold the Lamb of God: behold Him Who taketh away the sins of the world.

(three times)

P. Domine, non sum dignus, ut intres sub tectum meum; sed tantum dic verbo et sanabitur anima mea.

Lord, I am not worthy that Thou shouldst enter under my roof: say but the word and my soul shall be healed.

The celebrant places the Host on the tongue of the communicants, saying:

Corpus Domini nostri Jesu Christi custodiat animam tuam in vitam æternam. Amen.

May the body of Our Lord Jesus Christ keep thy soul unto life everlasting. Amen.

After the Communion of the Faithful, the celebrant receives into the chalice a small quantity of wine and says:

Quod ore sumpsimus, Domine, pura mente capiamus: et de munere temporali fiat nobis remedium sempiternum.

Into a pure heart, O Lord, may we receive the heavenly food which has passed our lips; bestowed upon us in time, may it be the healing of our souls for eternity.

The celebrant consumes the ablution, goes to the Epistle side where wine and water are poured over his fingers into the chalice, and says:

Corpus tuum, Domine, quod sumpsi, et sanguis, quem potavi, adhæreat visceribus meis; et præsta, ut in me non remaneat scelerum macula, quem pura

May Thy body, O Lord, which I have received, and Thy blood, which I have drunk, cleave to mine inmost parts: and do Thou grant that no stain of sin remain

et sancta refecerunt sacramenta. Qui vivis et regnas in sæcula sæculorum. Amen.

in me, whom pure and holy mysteries have refreshed. Who livest and reignest world without end. Amen.

THE COMMUNION (*In solemn Mass the subdeacon rearranges the chalice with its appurtenances and carries it to the credence table.*)

I. Cor. xi, 26-27. Quotiescumque manducabitis panem hunc, et calicem bibetis, mortem Domini annuntiabitis donec veniat: itaque quicumque manducaverit panem hunc, vel biberit calicem Domini indigne, reus erit corporis et sanguinis Domini.

I. Cor. xi, 26-27. As often as ye shall eat this bread, and drink the chalice, ye shall show forth the death of the Lord, until He come: therefore whosoever shall eat this bread or drink the chalice of the Lord unworthily, shall be guilty of the body and blood of the Lord.

Coming again to the middle of the altar, the celebrant kisses it, genuflects, turns to the people and salutes them with the words:
Stand

P. Dominus vobiscum.

The Lord be with you.

R. Et cum spiritu tuo.

And with thy spirit.

THE POSTCOMMUNION *Returning to the Missal, the celebrant sings:*

FAC nos, quaesumus Domine, divinitatis tuae sem-

GRANT us, O Lord, we beseech Thee, that in the life

piterna fruitione repleri: quam pretiosi corporis et sanguinis tui temporalis perceptio præfigurat: Qui vivis et regnas cum Deo Patre in unitate Spiritus Sancti, Deus, per omnia sæcula sæculorum. Amen.

everlasting we may have that full enjoyment of Thy Godhead which is foreshown by Thy precious body and blood, which we receive in this present life; Who livest and reignest with God the Father in the unity of the Holy Ghost, God, world without end. Amen.

The celebrant again kisses the altar, genuflects, turns to the people and salutes them with the words:

P. Dominus vobiscum.

The Lord be with thee.

R. Et cum spiritu tuo.

And with thy spirit.

P. Ite, missa est.

Go, the Mass is finished.

(In solemn Mass the deacon sings the Ite, Missa est)

R. Deo gratias.

Thanks be to God.

(Or, if there was no Gloria):

P. Benedicamus Domino.

Let us bless the Lord.

R. Deo gratias.

Thanks be to God.

Bowing down over the altar, the celebrant says:

Kneel

Placeat tibi sancta Trinitas, obsequium servitutis meæ, et

May the lowly homage of my service be pleasing to Thee,

Page 67

præsta, ut sacrificium, quod oculis tuæ majestatis indignus obtuli, tibi sit acceptabile, mihique et omnibus, pro quibus illud obtuli, sit, te miserante, propitiabile. Per Christum Dominum nostrum. Amen.

O most holy Trinity: and do Thou grant that the sacrifice which I, all unworthy, have offered up in the sight of Thy majesty may be acceptable to Thee and, because of Thy loving-kindness, may avail to atone to Thee for myself, and for all those for whom I have offered it up. Through Christ our Lord. Amen.

The celebrant kisses the altar, raises his hands and eyes to heaven, saying:

Benedicat vos omnipotens Deus—

May almighty God bless you—

Turning to the people, he blesses them, saying:

Pater, et Filius, ✠ et Spiritus Sanctus.
R. Amen.

The Father, and the Son, ✠ and the Holy Ghost.
Amen.

THE LAST GOSPEL *Going to the Gospel side of the altar, the celebrant says:*

Stand

P. Dominus vobiscum.

The Lord be with you.

R. Et cum spiritu tuo.

And with thy spirit.

Making the Sign of the Cross upon the altar, (if the Blessed Sacrament is on the table of the altar he omits this first Sign of the Cross) then upon his forehead, his lips, and his heart, he says:

P. Initium sancti Evangelii secundum Joannem.

The beginning of the holy Gospel according to St. John.

R. Gloria tibi, Domine.

In principio erat Verbum, et Verbum erat apud Deum, et Deus erat Verbum. Hoc erat in principio apud Deum. Omnia per ipsum facta sunt, et sine ipso factum est nihil quod factum est. In ipso vita erat, et vita erat lux hominum: et lux in tenebris lucet, et tenebræ eam non comprehenderunt. Fuit homo missus a Deo, cui nomen erat Joannes. Hic venit in testimonium, ut testimonium perhiberet de lumine, ut omnes crederent per illum. Non erat ille lux, sed ut testimonium perhiberet de lumine. Erat lux vera quæ illuminat omnem hominem venientem in hunc mundum. In mundo erat, et mundus per ipsum factus est, et mundus eum non cognovit. In propria venit, et sui eum

Glory be to Thee. O Lord.

In the beginning was the Word, and the Word was with God, and the Word was God. The same was in the beginning with God. All things were made by Him: and without Him was made nothing that was made. In Him was life, and the life was the light of men: and the light shineth in darkness, and the darkness did not comprehend it. There was a man sent from God, whose name was John. This man came for a witness, to give testimony of the light, that all men might believe through him. He was not the light, but was to give testimony of the light. That was the true light which enlighteneth every man that cometh into this world. He was in the world, and the world was made by

non receperunt. Quotquot autem receperunt eum, dedit eis potestatem filios Dei fieri, his qui credunt in nomine ejus. Qui non ex sanguinibus, neque ex voluntate carnis, neque ex voluntate viri, sed ex Deo nati sunt.

Him, and the world knew Him not. He came unto His own, and His own received Him not. But as many as received Him, to them He gave power to become the sons of God, to them that believe in His name. Who are born, not of blood, nor of the will of the flesh, nor of the will of man, but of God.

Kneel ET VERBUM CARO FACTUM EST, et habitavit in nobis (et vidimus gloriam ejus, gloriam quasi unigeniti a Patre), plenum gratiæ et veritatis.
 R. Deo gratias.

AND 'THE WORD WAS MADE FLESH, and dwelt among us (and we saw His glory, the glory as of the only-begotten of the Father), full of grace and truth.
 Thanks be to God.

All Kneel

THE PROCESSION

After the last Gospel, the celebrant takes off the chasuble and puts on the cope. He then goes to the altar and incenses the Blessed Sacrament. After the incensation he receives the humeral veil about his shoulders and, ascending to the altar, takes the Ostensorium in his hands and turns toward the people. (If there are three Ministers, the Deacon puts the veil about the celebrant's shoulders and places the Ostensorium in his hands.)
As soon as the celebrant turns toward the people, the procession is begun and the hymn, Pange Lingua (Sing, my tongue) is intoned.

THE INCENSATION OF THE BLESSED
SACRAMENT BEFORE THE PROCESSION.

Page 71

Out of reverence to our Eucharistic King, the celebrant carries the Blessed Sacrament under a canopy borne by priests or distinguished laymen.
During the procession the bells of the church are rung as a sign of rejoicing.

PANGE LINGUA

(This beautiful hymn was written by Saint Thomas Aquinas for the Office of the Feast of Corpus Christi.)

1.

Pange lingua gloriosi!

Corporis mysterium,

Sanguinisque pretiosi,

Quem in mundi pretium,

Fructus ventris generosi
Rex effudit gentium.

1.

Sing, my tongue, the Saviour's glory,
Of His flesh the mystery sing:
Of the blood, all price exceeding,
Shed by our immortal King.
Destined, for the world's redemption,
From a noble womb to spring.

2.

Nobis datus, nobis natus
Ex intacta virgine,

Et in mundo conversatus
Sparso verbi semine,

Sui moras incolatus

Miro clausit ordine.

2.

Of a pure and spotless Virgin
Born for us on earth below,
He, as man with man conversing,
Stay'd the seeds of truth to sow;
Then He clos'd in solemn order
Wondrously His life of woe.

THE CHANTING OF THE "PANGE LINGUA."
THE PROCESSION OF THE BLESSED
SACRAMENT.

3.

In supremae nocte coenae
Recumbens cum fratribus.
Observata lege plene

Cibis in legalibus,

Cibum turbae duodenae
Se dat suis manibus.

3.

On the night of that last Supper,
Seated with His chosen band,
He, the Paschal Victim eating,
First fulfills the law's command:
Then as food to all His brethren
Gives Himself with His own hand.

4.

Verbum caro panem verum
Verbo carnem efficit:

Fitquesanguis Christi merum.
Et si sensus deficit:

Ad firmandum cor sincerum
Sola fides sufficit.

4.

Word made flesh the bread of nature,
By His word to flesh He turns;
Wine into His blood He changes:
What though sense no change discerns.
Only be the heart in earnest,
Faith her lesson quickly learns.

When the celebrant returns to the altar, the ostensorium is placed on the throne (this is done by the deacon if there are three ministers) and the choir sings the last two verses of the Pange Lingua.

5.

Tantum ergo sacramentum
Veneremur cernui:

5.

Down in adoration falling,
Lo! the sacred Host we hail;

PROCESSION OF THE BLESSED SACRAMENT

Et antiquum docu-mentum,	Lo! o'er ancient forms departing
Novo cedat ritui:	Newer rites of grace prevail:
Praestet fides supple-mentum	Faith for all defects supplying
Sensuum defectui.	Where the feeble senses fail.

Here the Blessed Sacrament is incensed.

Genitori Genitoque	To the everlasting Father,
Laus et jubilatio,	And the Son who reigns on high,
Salus, honor, virtus quoque	With the Holy Ghost proceeding
Sit et benedictio,	Forth from each eternally,
Procedenti ab utro-que	Be salvation, honor, blessing,
Compar sit laudatio.	Might and endless majesty.
Amen.	Amen.

At the conclusion of the Tantum Ergo, the chanters (or the celebrant if there be no chanters) intone the Litany of the Saints; the sacred ministers or the choir responding.

The Litany of the Saints, in which the whole Court of Heaven is called upon to succor the Church and her children, is most appropriate during the Forty-Hours' Prayer which is, as we have seen, a cry of distress rising up to God from the afflicted souls of men.

KYRIE eleison. Christe eleison	LORD have mercy. Christ have mercy
Kyrie eleison.	Lord have mercy.
Christe audi nos.	Christ, hear us.

Christe exaudi nos.	Christ, graciously hear us.
Pater de caelis Deus,	God the Father of Heaven,
Miserere nobis.	*Have mercy on us.*
Fili Redemptor mundi Deus,	God the Son, Redeemer of the world,
Spiritus sancte Deus,	God the Holy Ghost,
Sancta Trinitas unus Deus,	Holy Trinity, one God,

Sancta Maria,		Holy Mary,	
Sancta Dei Génitrix,		Holy Mother of God,	
Sancta Virgo Virginum,	*Ora pro nobis.*	Holy Virgin of virgins,	
Sancte Michael,		St. Michael,	
Sancte Gabriel,		St. Gabriel,	
Sancte Raphael,		St. Raphael,	

Omnes sancti Angeli et Archangeli, *orate pro nobis.*	All ye Holy Angels and Archangels,	
Omnes sancti beatorum spirituum ordines, *orate pro nobis.*	All ye Holy Orders of Blessed Spirits.	*Pray for us*
Sancte Joannes Baptista, *ora pro nobis.*	St. John the Baptist,	
Sancte Joseph, *ora pro nobis.*	St. Joseph,	
Omnes sancti Papatriárchæ et Prophetæ, *orate pro nobis.*	All ye Holy Patriarchs and Prophets,	

Sancte Petre,	St. Peter,
Sancte Paule,	St. Paul,
Sancte Andréa,	St. Andrew,
Sancte Jacobe,	St. James,
Sancte Joánnes,	St. John,
Sancte Thoma,	St. Thomas,
Sancte Jacóbe,	St. James
Sancte Philíppe,	St. Philip,
Sancte Bartholo-mæe,	St. Bartholomew,
Sancte Matthæe,	St. Matthew,
Sancte Simon,	St. Simon,
Sancte Thaddæe,	St. Thaddeus,
Sancte Matthía,	St. Matthias,
Sancte Bárnaba,	St. Barnabas,
Sancte Lúca,	St. Luke,
Sancte Marce,	St. Mark,

Ora pro nobis. — *Pray for us*

Omnes sancti Apóstoli et Evagelistæ, *orate pro nobis.* — All ye Holy Apostles and Evangelists,

Omnes sancti Discípuli Domini, *orate pro nobis.* — All ye Holy Disciples of the Lord,

Omnes sancti Innocentes, *orate pro nobis.* — All ye Holy Innocents,

Sancte Stephane, *ora pro nobis.* — St. Stephen,

Sancte Laurenti, *ora pro nobis.* — St. Lawrence,

Sancte Vincenti, *ora pro nobis.* — St. Vincent,

Sancti Fabiane et Sebastiane, *orate pro nobis.* — SS. Fabian and Sebastian,

Sancti Joannes et Paule, *orale pro nobis.*	SS. John and Paul,	
Sancti Cosma et Damiane, *orale pro nobis.*	SS. Cosmas and Damian,	
Sancti Gervasi et Protasi, *orale pro nobis.*	SS. Gervase and Protase,	
Omnes sancti Martyres, *orale pro nobis.*	All ye holy Martyrs,	
Sancte Silvester,	St. Silvester,	
Sancte Gregori,	St. Gregory,	
Sancte Ambrosi,	St. Ambrose,	
Sancte Augustine,	St. Augustine,	
Sancte Hieronyme,	St. Jerome,	
Sancte Martine,	St. Martin,	
Sancte Nicolae,	St. Nicholas,	
Omnes sancti Pontifices et Confessores, *orale pro nobis.*	All ye holy Bishops and Confessors,	
Omnes sancti Doctores, *orale pro nobis.*	All ye holy Doctors,	
Sancte Antoni,	St. Antony,	
Sancte Benedicte,	St. Benedict,	
Sancte Bernarde,	St. Bernard,	
Sancte Dominice,	St. Dominic,	
Sancte Francisce,	St. Francis,	
Omnes sancti Sacerdotes et Levitae, *orale pro nobis.*	All ye holy Priests and Levites,	
Omnes sancti monachi et eremitae, *orale pro nobis.*	All ye holy monks and hermits,	

Ora pro nobis (first group)

Ora pro nobis (second group)

Pray for us

Sancta Maria Magdalena,		St. Mary Magdalen,
Sancta Agatha,	*Ora pro nobis*	St. Agatha,
Sancta Lucia,		St. Lucy,
Sancta Agnes,		St. Agnes,
Sancta Caecilia,		St. Cecilia,
Sancta Catharina,		St. Catharine,
Sancta Anastasia,		St. Anastasia,

Pray for us

Omnes sanctae virgines et viduae, *orate pro nobis.*

All ye holy virgins and widows,

Omnes sancti et sanctæ Dei, *intercedite pro nobis.*

All ye holy men and women, saints of God, *make intercession for us.*

Propitius esto, *parce nobis, Domine.*

Be merciful, *spare us, O Lord.*

Propitius esto, *exaudi nos, Domine.*

Be merciful *graciously hear us, O Lord.*

Ab omni málo,

From all evil,

Ab omni peccáto,

From all sin,

Ab ira tua,

From Thy wrath,

Ab imminéntibus perículis,

From the dangers that threaten,

A flagéllo terræ mótus,

From the scourge of earthquakes,

A peste, fame, et béllo,

From plague, famine and war,

A subitánea, et improvisa mórte

From sudden and unlooked-for death,

Ab insídiis diáboli,

From the snares of the devil,

Libera nos Domine

Ab ira, et ódio, et omni mala voluntáte,

From anger, hatred, and all ill-will,

A spíritu fornicatiónis,

From the spirit of fornication,

O Lord, deliver us

A fúlgure et tem-
pestáte,
A morte perpétua,

Per mystérium
sanctae Incarna-
tiónis tuæ,
Per adventum
tuum,
Per Nativitatem
tuam,
Per Baptísmum et
sanctum Jejun-
ium tuum,
Per Crucem et pas-
siónem tuam,
Per Mortem et
S e p u l t ú r a m
tuam,
Per Sanctam
Resurrectiónem
tuam,
Per admirabilem
Ascensiónem
tuam,
Per adventum
Spiritus Sancti
Parácliti,
In die judícii,

Libera nos Domine

From lightning
and tempest,
From everlasting
death,
By the mystery of
Thy Holy In-
carnation,
By Thy Coming,

By Thy Birth,

By Thy Baptism
and Holy Fast-
ing,
By Thy Cross and
Passion,
By Thy Death and
Burial,

By Thy Holy Re-
surrection,

By Thy Admirable
Ascension,

By the coming of
the Holy Ghost,
the Comforter,
In the day of judg-
ment,

O Lord, deliver us

Peccatóres,
Ut nobis parcas,

Ut nobis indúlgeas,

Ut ad véram poeni-
téntiam nos

Te rogamus, audi nos

We sinners,
That Thou wouldst
spare us,
That Thou wouldst
pardon us,
That Thou wouldst
bring us to true

We beseech Thee, hear us

perdúcere dig-
neris,

Ut Ecclésiam tuam
sanctam régere
et conserváre
dignéris.

Ut domnum apos-
tolicum, et
omnes ecclesias-
ticos ordines in
sancta religione
conservare dig-
neris,

Ut inimicos sanctae
ecclesiae humi-
liare digneris,

Ut regibus et prin-
cipibus christia-
nis pacem et ve-
ram concordiam
donare digneris,

Ut cuncto populo
christiano pacem
et unitatem lar-
giri digneris,

Ut omnes errantes
ad unitatem Ec-
clesiae revocare,
et infideles uni-
versos ad Evan-
gelii lumen per-
ducere digneris,

Te rogamus, audi nas

repentance,

That Thou wouldst
vouchsafe to gov-
ern and preserve
Thy Holy
Church,

That Thou wouldst
vouchsafe to pre-
serve our apos-
tolic prelate, and
all orders of the
Church in holy
religion,

That Thou wouldst
vouchsafe to
humble the ene-
mies of holy
Church,

That Thou wouldst
vouchsafe to
give peace and
true concord to
Christian kings
and princes,

That Thou wouldst
vouchsafe to
grant peace and
unity to all
Christian people,

That Thou wouldst
vouchsafe to re-
call all wander-
ers to the unity
of the Church,
and to lead all
unbelievers to

We beseech Thee, hear us

the Gospel light,

Ut nosmetipsos in tuo sancto servitio confortare et conservare digneris,	That Thou wouldst vouchsafe to confirm and preserve us in Thy holy service.
Ut mentes nostras ad caelestia desideria erigas,	That Thou wouldst lift up our minds to heavenly desires,
Ut omnibus benefactoribus nostris sempiterna bona retribuas,	That Thou wouldst reward all our benefactors with eternal blessings,
Ut animas nostras, fratrum, propinquorum et benefactorum nostrorum ab aeterna damnatione eripias,	That Thou deliver our souls, and the souls of our brethren, relatives and benefactors from eternal damnation,
Ut fructus terrae dare et conservare digneris,	That Thou wouldst vouchsafe to give and preserve the fruits of the earth,
Ut omnibus fidelibus defunctis requiem aeternam donare digneris,	That Thou wouldst vouchsafe to grant eternal rest to all the faithful departed,
Ut nos exaudire digneris,	That Thou wouldst vouchsafe graciously to hear us,
Fili Dei,	Son of God,

Te rogamus, audi nas

We beseech Thee, hear us

Agnus Dei, qui tollis peccata mundi, *parce nobis, Domine.*

Agnus Dei, qui tollis peccata mundi, *exaudi nos, Domine.*

Agnus Dei, qui tollis peccata mundi, *miserere nobis.*

Christe, audi nos.
Christe, exaudi nos.

Kyrie eléison.
Christe eleison.
Kyrie eléison.
Pater Noster (*secreto*)
V. Et ne nos inducas in tentationem.
R. Sed libera nos a malo.

PSALM 69

Deus, in adjutorium meum inténde: Domine ad adjuvandum me festína.

Confundantur et revereántur: qui quærunt ánimam meam.

Avertántur retrorsum et erubéscant:

Lamb of God, who takest away the sins of the world, *spare us, O Lord.*

Lamb of God, who takest away the sins of the world, *graciously hear us, O Lord.*

Lamb of God, who takest away the sins of the world, *have mercy on us.*

Christ, hear us,
Christ, graciously hear us.

Lord, have mercy.
Christ, have mercy.
Lord, have mercy.
Our Father (*in secret*)
And lead us not into temptation.
But deliver us from evil.

PSALM 69

O God, come to mine assistance. O Lord, make haste to help me.

Let them be confounded and ashamed: that seek after my soul.

Let them be turned backward, and blush

qui volunt mihi mala.

Avertántur statim erubescéntes: qui dicunt mihi: Euge, euge.

Exúltent et læténtur in te omnes qui quærunt te: et dicant semper: Magnificetur Dominus, qui diligunt salutáre tuum.

Ego vero egénus et pauper sum: Deus, adjúva me.

Adjutor meus, et liberátor meus es tu: Domine, ne moréris.

Gloria Patri et Filio et Spiritui Sancto.

Sicut erat in principio et nunc et semper et in sæcula sæculorum. Amen.

V. Salvos fac servos tuos.

R. Deus meus, sperántes in te.

V. Esto nobis Domine, turris fortitudinis.

for shame; that desire evils unto me.

Let them be straightway turned backward, blushing for shame, that say unto me: "'Tis well, 'tis well."

Let all that seek Thee rejoice and be glad in Thee: and let such as love Thy salvation say always, the Lord be magnified.

But I am needy and poor: O God, help me.

Thou art my helper and my deliverer: O Lord, do not delay.

Glory be to the Father and to the Son and to the Holy Ghost.

As it was in the beginning is now and ever shall be, world without end. Amen.

Save Thy servants.

Who hope in Thee, O my God.

Be unto us, O Lord, a tower of strength.

R. A facie inimici.

V. Nihil proficiat inimicus in nobis.

R. Et filius iniquitatis non apponat nocere nobis.

V. Domine, non secundum peccata nostra facias nobis.

R. Neque secundum iniquitates nostras retribuas nobis.

V. Oremus pro Pontifice nostro N.

R. Dominus conservet eum, et vivificet eum, et beatum faciat eum in terra, et non tradat eum in animam inimicorum ejus.

V. Oremus pro benefactoribus nostris.

R. Retribuere dignare, Domine, omnibus nobis bona facientibus propter nomen tuum, vitam aeternam. Amen.

V. Oremus pro fidelibus defunctis.

R. Requiem aeternam dona eis, Domine, et lux perpetua luceat eis.

From the face of the enemy.

Let not the enemy prevail against us.

Nor the son of iniquity have power to hurt us.

O Lord, deal not with us according to our sins.

Nor requite us according to our iniquities.

Let us pray for our Pontiff N.

The Lord preserve him, and give him life, and make him blessed upon earth, and deliver him not to the will of his enemies.

Let us pray for our benefactors.

Vouchsafe, O Lord, for Thy Name's sake, to reward with eternal life all them that do us good. Amen.

Let us pray for the faithful departed.

Grant them eternal rest, O Lord, and let light everlasting shine upon them.

V. Requiescant in pace.

R. Amen.

V. Pro fratribus nostris absentibus.

R. Salvos fac servos tuos, Deus meus, sperantes in te.

V. Mitte eis, Domine, auxilium de sancto.

R. Et de Sion tuere eos.

V. Domine, exaudi orationem meam.

R. Et clamor meus ad te veniat.

May they rest in peace.

Amen.

For our absent brethren.

·Save Thy servants who hope in Thee, O my God.

Send them help, O·Lord, from Thy holy place.

And from Sion protect them.

O Lord, hear my prayer.

And let my cry come unto Thee.

At the exposition (first day) the Dominus vobiscum and the prayers follow immediately. At the reposition (last day), the procession takes place at this point, and is followed by the singing of the Tantum Ergo. Then follows:

V. Panem de coelo praestitisti eis.

R. Omne delectamentum in se habentem.

Thou gavest them bread from heaven.

Having in itself every delight.

The celebrant rises and sings:

V. Dominus vobiscum.

R. Et cum spiritu tuo.

Oremus.

The Lord be with you.

And with thy spirit.

Let us pray.

DEUS, qui nobis sub sacramento mirabili, passionis tuæ memoriam reliquisti: tribue, quæsumus, ita nos corporis et sanguinis tui sacra mysteria venerari, ut redemptionis tuæ fructum in nobis jugiter sentiamus.

O GOD, Who in this wonderful sacrament, hast left us a memorial of Thy passion; grant us, we beseech Thee, so to venerate the sacred mysteries of Thy body and blood, that we may ever feel within us the fruit of Thy redemption.

(From Advent to Christmas)

Deus, qui de beatæ Mariæ Virginis utero Verbum tuum, Angelo nuntiante, carnem suscipere voluisti; præsta supplicibus tuis; ut qui vere eam Genitricem Dei credimus, ejus apud te intercessionibus adjuvemur.

O God, who didst will that Thy word, at the message of an angel, should take flesh in the womb of the Blessed Blessed Virgin Mary; grant that Thy petitioners, who verily believe her to be the Mother of God, may be assisted by her intercessions with Thee.

(From Christmas to the Purification)

Deus, qui salutis æternæ, beatæ Mariæ Virginitate foecunda, humano generi præmia præstitísti; tribue quæsumus; ut ipsam pro nobis

O God, who by the fruitful virginity of Blessed Mary, hast given to mankind the rewards of eternal salvation; grant, we beseech Thee, that

intercédere sentiámus, per quam merúimus auctorem vitæ suscípere, Dominum nostrum Jesum Christum Filium tuum.

we may experience the intercession of her, by whom we have deserved to receive the Author of Life, our Lord Jesus Christ, Thy Son.

(From the Purification to Advent)

Concéde nos famulos tuos, quæsumus, Domine Deus, perpétua mentis et corporis sanitáte gaudére; et gloriósa beatæ Mariæ semper Virginis intercessióne a præsenti liberári tristítia, et æterna perfrui lætítia.

Grant, we beseech Thee, O Lord God, that we, Thy servants, may enjoy perpetual health of mind and body; and, by the glorious intercession of the Blessed Mary, ever Virgin, may be delivered from present sorrow, and possess eternal joy.

Omnipotens sempitérne Deus, miserére famulo tuo Pontifici nostro, N., et dírige eum secundum tuam cleméntiam in viam salútis ætérnæ; ut te donante tibi plácita cúpiat, et tota virtúte perfíciat.

O Almighty God, have mercy on Thy servant, N., our Sovereign Pontiff, and direct him according to Thy clemency, in the way of everlasting salvation, that by Thy grace he may desire things that are pleasing to Thee and perform them with all his strength.

Deus, refúgium nostrum et virtus, adésto piis Ecclesiæ tuae précibus, auctor ipse pietátis: et præsta, ut quod fidéliter pétimus, efficáciter consequámur.

O God, our refuge and our strength, and the author of all goodness, give ear to the pious prayers of Thy Church, and grant that what we faithfully ask, we may effectually obtain.

Omnipotens, sempitérne Deus, qui salvas omnes, et néminem vis períre: réspice ad ánimas, diabólica fraude decéptas; ut omni haeretica pravitáte depósita, errántium corda resipíscant, et ad veritátis tuæ rédeant unitátem.

O Almighty, everlasting God, who savest all and wishest none to perish: look on the souls deceived by the wiles of the evil one that, all the pravity of heresy being laid aside, the hearts of those in error may repent and return to the unity of Thy truth.

Omnipotens sempiterne Deus, qui vivorum dominaris simul et mortuorum, omniùmque misereris, quos tuos fide et opere futuros esse prænoscis: te supplices exoramus; ut, pro quibus effundere preces decrevimus quos-

Almighty and everlasting God, who hast dominion over the living and the dead, and art merciful to all whom Thou foreknowest shall be Thine by faith and good works; we humbly beseech Thee that they for

que vel praesens saeculum adhuc in carne retinet, vel futurum jam exutos corpore suscepit, intercedentibus omnibus Sanctis tuis, pietatis tuae clementia omnium delictorum suorum veniam consequantur. Per Dominum nostrum Jesum Christum Filium tuum, qui tecum vivit et regnat in unitate Spiritus Sancti Deus, per omnia saecula saeculorum.

R. Amen.

whom we intend to pour forth our prayers, whether this present world still detain them in the flesh, or the world to come hath already received them out of their bodies, may, through the intercession of all Thy saints, by the clemency of Thy goodness, obtain the remission of all their sins. Through our Lord, Jesus Christ, Thy Son, who with Thee liveth and reigneth in the unity of the Holy Ghost, God, world without end.

Amen.

The celebrant kneels and sings:

V. Domine exaudi orationem meam.

R. Et clamor meus ad te veniat.

V. Exaudiat nos omnipotens et misericors Dominus.

R. Et custodiat nos semper. Amen.

V. Fidelium animae per misericor-

Lord, hear my prayer.

And let my cry come unto thee.

May the almighty and merciful Lord graciously hear us.

And ever preserve us. Amen.

May the souls of the faithful, through

diam-Dei requiescant   the mercy of God,
in pace.   rest in peace.
   R. Amen.   Amen.

When the Litany is finished the clergy retire to the sacristy.

During the hours of Exposition, our Eucharistic Lord must never be left without adorers. (Prayers for visits will be found at the end of this booklet.)

EVENING SERVICE When the Exposition is interrupted during the night, as is the custom in this country, the evening devotions usually consist of prayer, sermon, hymns and benediction according to the instruction of the Bishop of the diocese.

THE SECOND DAY

THE MASS *The Mass celebrated on the second day is the solemn Mass for Peace (unless some other is ordered). The color of the vestments is violet in accord with the note of humility and pleading sounded in the Mass. Unless necessity requires it, this Mass is not celebrated at the altar of Exposition but at a side altar. If possible, Holy Communion is not distributed from the altar at which this Mass is said nor from the altar of Exposition, but from some other, in the tabernacle of which the Blessed Sacrament is reserved.*

THE ORDINARY OF THE MASS *The Ordinary is the same as in the Mass of the first day with the exceptions indicated. (See page 15.)*

THE PROPER PRAYERS

The Proper prayers are as follows:

THE INTROIT

Eccli. xxxvi

DA pacem, Domine, sustinentibus te, ut prophetae tui fideles inveniantur: exaudi preces servi tui, et plebis tuae Israel. *Ps.* 121. Laetatus sum in his, quae dicta sunt mihi: in domum Domini ibimus. *V.* Gloria Patri, et Filio, et Spiritui Sancto: Sicut erat in principio, et

Ecclus. xxxvi

GIVE peace, O Lord, to them that patiently wait for Thee, that Thy prophets may be found faithful: hear the prayers of Thy servant, and of Thy people Israel. *Ps.* 121. I rejoiced at the things that were said to me: we shall go into the house of the Lord. *V.* Glory be to the Father, and to the Son, and to the Holy Ghost: as it was in the begin-

nunc et semper, et in saecula saeculorum. Amen.

ning, is now and ever shall be; world without end. Amen.

(The Gloria is omitted)

THE COLLECT

DEUS, a quo sancta desideria, recta consilia et justa sunt opera: da servis tuis illam, quam mundus dare non potest, pacem; ut et corda nostra mandatis tuis dedita, et, hostium sublata formidine, tempora sint, tua protectione, tranquilla. Per Dominum nostrum Jesum Christum, Filium Tuum, qui tecum vivit et regnat in unitate Spiritus Sancti, Deus, per omnia saecula saeculorum.

Amen.

O GOD, from whom are holy desires, right counsels, and just works; give to Thy servants that peace which the world cannot give; that our hearts may be disposed to obey Thy commandments, and the fear of enemies being removed, our times, by Thy protection, may be peaceful. Through our Lord Jesus Christ, Thy Son, Who liveth and reigneth with Thee in the unity of the Holy Ghost, God, world without end.

Amen.

THE EPISTLE

2 Mach. i, 1-5.
FRATRIBUS, qui sunt per Aegyptum, Judaeis, salutem

2 Mach. i.
TO the brethren, the Jews that are throughout Egypt;

tem dicunt fratres, qui sunt in Jerosolymis, Judaei, et qui in regione Judaeae, et pacem bonam. Benefaciat vobis Deus, et meminerit testamenti sui, quod locutus est ad Abraham, et Isaac, et Jacob, servorum suorum fidelium: et det vobis cor omnibus ut colatis eum, et faciatis ejus voluntatem, corde magno, et animo volenti. Adaperiat cor vestrum in lege sua, et in praeceptis suis, et faciat pacem. Exaudiat orationes vestras, et reconcilietur vobis, nec vos deserat in tempore malo, Dominus Deus noster.

the brethren, the Jews that are in Jerusalem, and in the land of Judea, send health and good peace. May God be gracious to you, and remember His covenant that He made with Abraham, and Isaac, and Jacob, His faithful servants. And give you all a heart to worship Him, and to do His will with a great heart, and a willing mind. May He open your heart in His law, and in His commandments, and send you peace. May He hear your prayers, and be reconciled unto you, and never forsake you in the evil time, the Lord our God.

THE GRADUAL

Ps. 121.

Rogate quae ad pacem sunt Jerusalem; et abundantia diligentibus te. *V.* Fiat pax in virtute tua, et abundantia

Ps. 121.

Pray ye for the things that are for the peace of Jerusalem: and abundance for them that love thee. *V.* Let

in turribus tuis. Alleluia, alleluia. V. Ps. 147, Lauda, Jerusalem, Dominum: lauda Deum tuum, Sion. Alleluia.

peace be in thy strength: and abundance in thy towers. Alleluia, alleluia. V. Ps. 147. Praise the Lord, O Jerusalem: praise thy God, O Sion. Alleluia.

After Septuagesima, instead of Alleluia and V., is said:

Tractus, Ps. 75. Notus in Judaea Deus, in Israel magnum nomen ejus. V. Et factus est in pace locus ejus, et habitatio ejus in Sion. V. Ibi confregit potentias arcuum, scutum, gladium, et bellum.

Tract. Ps. 75. In Judea God is known, His name is great in Israel. V. And His place is in peace, and His abode in Sion. V. There hath He broken the powers of bows, the shield, the sword and the battle.

At Eastertide, instead of the Gradual, is said:

Alleluja, alleluja. V. Ps. 147, 12. Lauda, Jerusalem, Dominum: lauda Deum tuum, Sion. Alleluja. V. Ibid., 14. Qui posuit fines tuos pacem, et adipe frumenti satiat te. Alleluja.

Alleluia, alleluia. V. Ps. 147, 12. Praise the Lord, O Jerusalem: praise thy God, O Sion. Alleluia. V. Ibid., 14. Who hath set peace for thy borders, and satisfieth thee with the fat of wheat. Alleluia.

Sequentia Sancti Evangelii Secundum Joannem. (*Joann.* xx, 19-23.)

IN illo tempore: Dum sero esset illo die, una sabbatorum, et fores essent clausae, ubi erant discipuli congregati propter metum Judæorum: venit Jesus et stetit in medio, et dixit eis: Pax vobis. Et cum hoc dixisset ostendit eis manus, et latus. Gavisi sunt ergo discipuli, viso Domino. Dixit ergo eis iterum: Pax vobis. Sicut misit me Pater, et ego mitto vos. Haec cum dixisset, insufflavit, et dixit eis: Accipite Spiritum

The continuation of the Holy Gospel according to Saint John. (xx, 19-23.)

AT that time:when it was late, that same day, the first of the week, and the doors were shut, where the disciples were gathered together for fear of the Jews, Jesus came and stood in the midst, and said to them: Peace be to you. And when He had said this, He showed them his hands and His side. The disciples therefore were glad, when they saw the Lord. He said therefore to them again: Peace be to you. As the Father hath sent Me, I also send you. When He had said this, He breathed on them; and He said to them: Receive ye the Holy Ghost. Whose sins you shall

Sanctum: quorum re-
miseritis peccata, re-
mittuntur eis: et
quorum retinueritis,
retenta sunt.

forgive, they are for-
given them; and
whose sins you shall
retain, they are re-
tained.

The Credo is said. (*See page* 32.)

THE OFFERTORY

Psalm 134, 3-6.
Laudate Dominum,
quia benignus est:
psallite nomini ejus,
quoniam suave est:
omnia quaecumque
voluit, fecit in caelo
et in terra.

Ps. cxxxiv. Praise
ye the Lord, for He
is good, sing ye to
His name, for it is
sweet: whatsoever
He pleased, He hath
done in heaven and
upon earth.

THE SECRET

DEUS, qui creden-
tes in te popu-
los nullis sinis concuti
terroribus: dignare
preces et hostias dic-
tae tibi plebis sus-
cipere; ut pax a
tua pietate concessa,
christianorum fines
ab omni hoste faciat
esse securos. Per
Dominum nostrum,
Jesum Christum, Fil-
ium Tuum, qui Te-
cum vivit et regnat
in unitate Spiritus
Sancti, Deus, per

O GOD, who suf-
ferest not the
nations that believe
in Thee to be shaken
by any fear, deign,
we beseech Thee,
to receive the prayers
and sacrifices of the
people consecrated to
Thee, that peace, the
gift of Thy loving
kindness, may render
Chr'stian countries
safe from every
enemy. Through
Our Lord Jesus
Christ, Thy Son, who

omnia saecula saecu-
lorum. Amen.

liveth and reigneth
with Thee in the
unity of the Holy
Ghost, God, world
without end. Amen.

THE PREFACE

Vere dignum et jus-
tum est, æquum et
salutare, nos tibi sem-
per, et ubique gra-
tias agere: Domine
sancte, Pater omni-
potens, æterne Deus:
per Christum Do-
minum nostrum.

It is truly meet and
just, right and profit-
able for us, at all
times, and in all
places, to give thanks
to Thee, O Lord, the
holy One, the Father
almighty, the ever-
lasting God: through
Christ our Lord.

Per quem majesta-
tem tuam laudant
angeli, adorant do-
minationes, tremunt
potestates. Cœli,
cœlorumque virtutes,
ac beata seraphim,
socia exultatione con-
celebrant. Cum qui-
bus et nostras voces,
ut admitti jubeas,
deprecamur, supplici
confessione dicentes:

Through Whom
the angels praise, the
dominations adore,
the powers, trem-
bling with awe, wor-
ship Thy majesty:
which the heavens
and the forces of
heaven, together with
the blessed seraphim,
joyfully do magnify.
And do Thou com-
mand that it be per-
mitted to our lowli-
ness to join with
them in confessing
Thee and unceasingly
to repeat:

Sanctus, sanctus, sanctus Dominus Deus Sabaoth.

Pleni sunt cœli et terra gloria tua.

Hosanna in excelsis.

Benedictus qui venit in nomine Domini.

Hosanna in excelsis.

Holy, Holy, Holy, Lord God of hosts.

The heavens and the earth are full of Thy glory.

Hosanna in the highest.

Blessed is He that cometh in the name of the Lord.

Hosanna in the highest.

THE COMMUNION

Joann. xiv. 27. Pacem relinquo vobis: pacem meam do vobis, dicit Dominus.

John xiv 27. Peace I leave unto you, my peace I give you, saith the Lord.

THE POST COMMUNION

DEUS, auctor pacis et amator, quem nosse, vivere, cui servire, regnare est: protege ab omnibus impugnationibus supplices tuos; ut, qui in defensione tua confidimus, nullius hostilitatis arma timeamus. Per Dominum nostrum Jesum Christum, Filium Tuum, qui tecum vivit et regnat

OGOD, the author and lover of peace, to know whom is to live, to serve whom is to reign: shield Thy suppliants from all assaults, so that we who trust in Thy protection may fear no foe. Through our Lord Jesus Christ, Thy Son, who liveth and reigneth in the unity of the Holy

in unitate Spiritus Sancti, Deus, per omnia saecula saeculorum.

Ghost, God, world without end.

Amen.

Amen.

(In Eastertide, Alleluia is added to the Offertory and Communion of the above Mass; and a twofold Alleluia to the Introit.)

THE THIRD DAY

THE MASS *The Mass celebrated on the third day is the same as that of the first day. (See page 15.)*

CLOSING *After the Last Gospel, the celebrant takes off* **CEREMONIES** *the chasuble and puts on the cope. He then returns to the foot of the altar, where, with the sacred ministers (if the service be solemn) he kneels while the Litany of the Saints (see page 76) is chanted by the chanters (or by the celebrant, if there be no chanters) and the choir.*

After the prayer "Domine, exaudi orationem meam—Lord, hear my prayer," and its response, the celebrant incenses the Blessed Sacrament. This done, he receives the humeral veil about his shoulders, takes the monstrance in his hands, turns towards the people, and the procession begins. During the procession, the Pange Lingua is sung as on the first day. (See page 72). At the end of the procession the monstrance is again placed on the altar and the choir sings the Tantum Ergo. (See page 74.)
At the "Genitori" the Blessed Sacrament is incensed as usual.
At the end of the hymn the celebrant sings the versicle:

V. Panem de coelo praestitisti eis.

R. Omne delecta- mentum in se haben- tem.

Thou hast given them bread from heaven.

Replenished with all sweetness and de- light.

Then the celebrant rises and sings the prayers which follow the Litany of the Saints. (See page 84.) When the prayers are finished, Benediction is given in the usual manner, the Blessed Sacrament is replaced in the tabernacle, and the ceremony terminates. (It is quite the custom for the entire congregation to sing the Te Deum "Holy God, We Praise Thy Name" at the close of the services and the words of this hymn are herewith given:) Where the custom prevails of terminating the Devotion on the evening of the third day, the celebrant and ministers return to the sacristy as usual after Mass, and in the evening all the ceremonies prescribed above are observed.

Holy God, We Praise Thy Name.

1. Holy God, we praise Thy name,
   Lord of all, we bow before Thee!
All on earth Thy sceptre claim,
   All in heav'n above adore Thee.

BENEDICTION OF THE BLESSED SACRAMENT
AT THE CLOSING

Page 103

||Infinite Thy vast domain,
Everlasting is Thy reign.||

2. Hark! the loud celestial hymn,
   Angel choirs above are raising!
Cherubim and Seraphim,
   In unceasing chorus praising.

   ||Fill the heavens with sweet accord;
   Holy! Holy! Holy Lord.||

3. Lo! the apostolic train,
   Join Thy sacred name to hallow!
Prophets swell the loud refrain,
   And with white-robed martyrs follow.

   ||And from morn till set of sun,
   Through the Church the song goes on.||

PRAYERS AND READINGS FOR VISITS TO THE BLESSED SACRAMENT

"THE PRISONER OF LOVE."

PRAYERS AND READINGS FOR VISITS TO THE BLESSED SACRAMENT

During your visits to Jesus in the Blessed Sacrament, strive to be natural. Let your converse be that of friend with Friend. Do not bind yourself to any formula;—just speak to Jesus as your love prompts. Talk to Him of your joys and sorrows, of your hopes and fears, your needs and your desires. If you can not pray, then, kneel peacefully at the feet of Jesus confident that He understands everything far better than you could express it, and that He sympathizes with you with all the loving ardor of His Sacred Heart.

The following thoughts and prayers,* arranged for two half-hour visits in five-minute periods, but suitable also for the Holy Hour, are merely suggestive and may prove helpful to some souls.

FIRST HALF-HOUR
FIVE MINUTES.

Prostrate yourself before the Divine Majesty, veiled in the adorable Sacrament of the altar, and say from the depths of your soul:

O SACRAMENT most holy! O Sacrament divine!

All praise and all thanksgiving be every moment Thine!

(Indulgence of 100 days, once a day)

Read slowly: pause frequently and reflect.

O MY Eucharistic Jesus, I believe Thy divine word that under this appearance of bread, Thou Thyself art really present as Thou art in heaven.—I believe, O my Eucharistic Jesus, here present in the adorable Sacrament, that Thou art the same Jesus of Nazareth Who didst heal the sick,—and didst raise the dead,—and Who for us didst suffer,—and die upon the Cross.

*Taken from *The Blessed Sacrament Book*, by Father Lasance.

Look adoringly at the Sacred Host and say over and over with great faith and love:

Sacred Heart of Jesus, I trust in Thee.

(300 days indulgence each time)

My Lord and my God.

(7 years and 7 times 40 days indulgence each time)

Say with great devotion:

O JESUS, humbly kneeling in Thy presence and united with all the faithful on earth and all the Saints in heaven, I adore Thee true God and true man, here present in the Holy Eucharist. Grateful even to the very depths of my soul, I ove Thee with my whole heart, O Jesus, Who art infinitely perfect and infinitely amiable. Enrich me with Thy grace, so that I shall never in any way offend Thee; and thus strengthened here on earth by Thy Eucharistic presence may I merit to enjoy with Mary Thy eternal and blessed presence in heaven. Amen.

(Indulgence of 300 days once a day before the Blessed Sacrament)

EUCHARISTIC Heart of Jesus, have mercy on us.

(Indulgence of 300 days each time)

FIVE MINUTES.

Read slowly; pause frequently and reflect:

"COME to Me, all you that labor and are burdened, and I will refresh you."— Does not Jesus still address these words to us from His Sacrament of Love?—Come to Me, for nowhere else shall you find the rest you crave.—Come to Me. you sorrow-laden, for no one else can unde; tand your grief as I can.—I know the weight of your cross,— its special perplexities,—its aggravations.—

I know all the secret folds of your heart.—
Come to Me, then, with your griefs,—your
disappointments,—your secret sorrows,—your
fears,—your struggles,—your sins.—Come to
your Jesus, Whose Heart is ever open to
receive you and to shelter you.—Come to
Him Who compassionates all,—and Whose
Heart yearns to comfort all.—Come to Me
and you shall find rest to your souls.

O SWEETEST Heart of Jesus, I implore
That I may ever love Thee more and
more.

(Indulgence of 300 days each time)
* * *

Sweet is our Lord in thought, sweet in the
pages of the Holy Gospel, sweet in the shadowy
symbol or the devout picture, sweet yet more
in the holy crucifix, but sweeter beyond com-
parison in the Adorable Sacrament of His
Love. Wherefore the Church sings in the
words of her Saint:
Jesu! the very thought of Thee,
With sweetness fills my breast:
But sweeter far Thy face to see,
And in Thy presence rest. (Oakley)
* * *
Repeat frequently and devoutly the aspiration:

SWEET Heart of my Jesus, make me love
Thee more and more.
(Indulgence of 300 days each time)

FIVE MINUTES.
Read slowly and reflect.

JESUS, knowing that His hour was come,
that He should pass out of this world to
the Father, having loved His own who were

in the world, He loved them to the end. And so at the end came the Last Supper and the First Communion; for this jealous Lover could not bear to leave us without a keepsake, a love token, such as only God could imagine, such as only God could give.

* * *

DEAR Jesus, present in the Sacrament of the altar, be forever thanked and praised. Love worthy of all celestial and terrestrial love! Who, out of infinite love for me, ungrateful sinner, didst assume our human nature, didst shed Thy most precious blood in the cruel scourging, and didst expire on a shameful cross for our eternal welfare! Now illumined with lively faith, with the outpouring of my whole soul and the fervor of my heart, I humbly beseech Thee, through the infinite merits of Thy painful sufferings, give me strength and courage to destroy every evil passion which sways my heart, to bless Thee in my greatest afflictions, and to glorify Thee by the exact fulfilment of all my duties, supremely to hate all sin, and thus to become a saint.

(100 days indulgence once a day)

A Message from the Sacred Heart.

A Message from the Sacred Heart:
What may its message be?
"My child, My child, give Me thy heart—
My Heart has bled for thee."

This is the message Jesus sends
To my poor heart today,
And eager from His throne He bends
To hear what I shall say.

A message to the Sacred Heart:
Oh, bear it back with speed:
"Come, Jesus, reign within my heart—
Thy Heart is all I need."

Thus, Lord, I'll pray until I share
That home whose joy Thou art:
No message, dearest Jesus, there—
For heart will speak to Heart.
                    (Father Matthew Russell, S.J.)

SACRED Heart of Jesus, Thy kingdom come!

(300 days indulgence each time)

Five Minutes.
Read slowly and reflect.

Think how Jesus, with boundless liberality, opens today the infinite treasures of His Sacred Heart.—You are poor; come and be made rich.—You are ill; He will cure you.— Come if your heart is troubled and anxious; He will calm it.—Come, trembling, guilty soul; come and be pardoned.

JESUS, meek and humble of Heart, make my heart like unto Thine.

(300 days indulgence each time)

* * *

Speak to Jesus in the Adorable Sacrament; compassionate the sufferings of His passion and the shameful treatment He daily receives from men in the Sacrament of His Love. Men love Jesus so little. They neglect Him and leave Him alone in His lonely tabernacle while they give themselves over to lives of pleasure and sin. You wish to make reparation. The best means is to become very holy and pleasing to Jesus. Tell Him that you desire this, and really mean what you say.

* * *

MY God, my only good, Thou art all mine; grant that I may be all Thine.

(300 *days indulgence once a day*)

* * *

LISTEN to Jesus speaking to your soul:—
In order to expiate your own faults and in reparation for the outrages done Me in this adorable Sacrament, you must become filled with lively faith and profound respect toward My Majesty hidden behind these sacred veils. Everything about the altar must speak to you of this. The lamp which ever burns before Me tells you that I am present. The sanctuary, enclosed and silent, reminds you of My sanctity and union with God. The tabernacle tells you of My love of the hidden life. The purity of the sacred vessels warns you that I look for purity in your soul.

Reflect and make resolutions.

* * *

LET us with Mary Immaculate adore, thank, supplicate, and console the most Sacred and beloved Eucharistic Heart of Jesus.

(200 *days indulgence each time*)

* * *

Five Minutes.

In a spirit of reparation, recite the following:

JESUS, my God, my Saviour, true God and true Man, in that lowly homage with which the Faith itself inspires me, with my whole heart I adore and love Thee in the most august Sacrament of the Altar, in reparation for all the acts of irreverence, profanation and sacrilege, which I myself may ever have been so unhappy as to have committed, as well as for all such acts that ever have been done by others, or that may be done in ages yet to come. I adore Thee, my God, not indeed as Thou deservest, nor as much as I am bound to adore Thee, but as far as I am able; and I would that I could adore Thee with all the perfection of which a reasonable creature is capable. Meantime I purpose now and ever to adore Thee, not only for those Catholics who adore and love Thee not, but also for the conversion of all bad Christians, and of all heretics, schismatics, Mohammedans, Jews and idolaters. Jesus, my God, mayest Thou be ever known, adored, loved and praised every moment in the most holy and divine Sacrament. Amen.

I ADORE Thee every moment, O living bread of heaven, great Sacrament.

JESUS, treasure of Mary's heart, I pray Thee, send Thy blessing on my soul.

HOLIEST Jesus! loving Saviour! I give Thee my heart.
(200 days indulgence each time)

* * *

Look at the Sacred Host and recite very devoutly ten times the following ejaculation in reparation for the insults offered Jesus in the Blessed Sacrament.

JESUS, my God, I adore Thee here present in the Sacrament of Thy Love.
(100 days indulgence each time before the tabernacle)
(300 days indulgence each time before the Blessed Sacrament exposed)

OH! See upon the altar placed,
The Victim of the greatest love!
Let all the earth below adore,
And join the choirs of heaven above.
Sweet Sacrament, we thee adore:
Oh! make us love thee more and more.

Five Minutes.
Read slowly and reflect.

ALL that is good and pure in human love
is realized on a transcendent scale in the
love divine. There are many touching tales
in poetry, founded on the prose of real life,
telling how kings and princes assumed a
lowly disguise in order to win the true love of
lowly maidens who loved them for their own
sake and not for the rank and wealth which
they were startled and grieved to discover,
and from which they shrank when their royal
suitors insisted on raising them to their own
height and sharing everything with them. In
like manner the Divine Lover of our souls has
descended to our level, has disguised Himself
in our lowly human nature, that He may win
our familiar and tender love. He, too, will
elevate His low-born spouse to a crown of
heavenly glory.

* * *

DIVINE Jesus, Incarnate Son of God, Who
for our salvation didst vouchsafe to be
born in a stable, to pass Thy life in poverty,
trials, and misery, and to die amid the sufferings of the Cross, I entreat Thee, say to Thy
Divine Father at the hour of my death:
Father, forgive him; say to Thy beloved
Mother: Behold thy son; say to my soul: this
day thou shalt be with me in paradise. My

God, my God, forsake me not in that hour.
I thirst; yes, my God, my soul thirsts after
Thee, Who art the fountain of living waters.
My life passes like a shadow; yet a little
while, and all will be consummated. Wherefore, O my adorable Saviour, from this
moment for all eternity, into Thy hands I
commend my spirit. Lord Jesus, receive my
soul. Amen.

(Indulgence of 300 days each time)

SOUL of Christ, be my sanctification.
Body of Christ, be my salvation.
Blood of Christ, fill all my veins.
Water of Christ's side, wash out my stains.
Passion of Christ, my comfort be.
O good Jesus, listen to me.
In Thy wounds I fain would hide,
Ne'er to be parted from Thy side.
Guard me should the foe assail me.
Call me when my life shall fail me.
Bid me come to Thee above,
With Thy saints to sing Thy love,
World without end. Amen.

(300 days indulgence each time)

* * *

Close your visit with the following:
An Act of Spiritual Communion.

MY Jesus, I believe that Thou art in the
most holy Sacrament. I love Thee
above all things, and I long for Thee in my
soul. Since I can not receive Thee now sacra-
mentally, come at least spiritually into my
heart. I embrace Thee as already there and
unite myself wholly to Thee; never permit me
to be separated from Thee.

Jesus, my good, my sweet love, wound,

inflame this heart of mine so that it may be always and all on fire for Thee.

(Indulgence of 60 days once a day)

SECOND HALF-HOUR
THE EUCHARISTIC ROSARY

(In addition to the ordinary abundant Rosary Indulgences, a Plenary Indulgence, on the usual conditions, may be gained for reciting the Rosary before the Blessed Sacrament.)

Five Minutes.

THE SORROWFUL MYSTERIES:
First Mystery: The Agony in the Garden.

Divine Saviour, under the weight of sorrow and sadness caused by our sins, Thou fallest, bathed in a sweat of blood, and Thou endurest a mortal agony. In the Blessed Sacrament, also, Thou art still more humbled and annihilated on account of our sins.

We adore Thee and we compassionate Thy agony of suffering in the Garden of Gethsemane as well as Thy agony of humiliation in the Eucharist, and we beg of Thee, through the intercession of Thy holy Mother, a heartfelt sorrow for our sins.

Recite slowly and devoutly the first decade. Then for the souls in Purgatory, say the *De Profundis:*

Out of the depths I have cried unto Thee, O Lord: Lord, hear my voice.

Let Thine ears be attentive to the voice of my supplication.

If Thou, O Lord, wilt mark our iniquities: O Lord, who shall stand it?

For with Thee there is mercy: and by reason of Thy law I have waited on Thee, O Lord.

My soul hath waited on His word: my soul hath hoped in the Lord.

From the morning watch even unto night:
let Israel hope in the Lord.

For with the Lord there is mercy: and with
Him is plenteous redemption.

And He shall redeem Israel: from all his
iniquities.

V. Eternal rest give to them, O Lord.

R. And let perpetual light shine upon
them.

* * *

Five Minutes.

Second Mystery: The Scourging at the Pillar.

O Good Jesus! scourged and covered with
wounds, the sins committed by men against
the holy virtue of purity thus torture Thy
innocent flesh; and in the Blessed Sacrament
impure hearts insult Thee by their sacri-
legious communions.

O Thou bloody Victim, scourged at the
pillar, patient Victim, abused in the adorable
Sacrament of the altar, we adore Thee and we
beg of Thee, through the intercession of Thy
holy Mother, the grace of mortifying our
senses.

Recite slowly and devoutly the second decade. Then
say the *Anima Christi*:

SOUL of Christ, sanctify me.
Body of Christ, save me.
Blood of Christ, inebriate me.
Water from the side of Christ, wash me.
Passion of Christ, strengthen me.
O good Jesus, hear me.
Within Thy wounds hide me.
Permit me not to be separated from Thee.
From the malignant enemy defend me.
In the hour of my death call me,
And bid me come to Thee,

That with Thy saints I may praise Thee
Forever and ever.   Amen.
(Indulgence of 300 days every time)
* * *

Five Minutes.
Third Mystery: The Crowning with Thorns.

O King of Glory! crowned with thorns and
proclaimed in derision king of the Jews by
brutal soldiers who ignominiously spit upon
Thy adorable face, Thou fallest a victim to
the sins committed by pride; in the Blessed
Sacrament also Thou bearest a crown of
ignominy made up of the many acts of
irreverence, contempt, hypocrisy, and vanity
committed by Christians in Thy sanctuary.

O loving King! overwhelmed with insults
both in Thy passion and in the Sacred Host,
we adore Thee, and we beg of Thee, through
the intercession of Thy holy Mother, the
grace of mortifying our self-love.

Recite slowly and devoutly the third decade.   Then
ponder prayerfully over the following:

JESUS as though Thyself wert here,
   I draw in trembling sorrow near;
And, hanging o'er Thy form divine,
Kneel down to kiss these wounds of Thine.

Hail, awful brow! hail, thorny wreath!
Hail, countenance, now pale in death!
Whose glance but late so brightly blazed
That angels trembled as they gazed.

And hail to thee, my Saviour's side!
And hail to thee, thou wound so wide;
Thou wound more ruddy than the rose,
True antidote of all our woes!

Oh, by those sacred hands and feet
For me so mangled! I entreat,
My Jesu, turn me not away,
But let me here for ever stay.

(Fr. Caswall)

* * *

Five Minutes.
Fourth Mystery: The Carrying of the Cross.

Curses, outrages, ill-treatments, anguish of
heart, sufferings of all kinds can not alter,
O dear Redeemer, the mildness and patience
with which Thou carriest Thy heavy cross;
with like sweetness and patience dost Thou
bear in the long course of ages, doubts, want
of confidence, murmurs, insults, and dis-
couragement on the part of Thy children.

O Jesus! we adore Thee carrying with love
the cross prepared for Thee by Thy Father
and we beg of Thee, through the intercession of Thy holy Mother, patience in the
trials of this life.

Recite slowly and devoutly the fourth decade.   Then
ponder prayerfully over the following:

O THOU Mother! fount of love!
  Touch my spirit from above,
Make my heart with thine accord;
Make me feel as thou hast felt,
Make my soul to glow and melt
With the love of Christ, my Lord.

Holy mother! pierce me through;
In my heart each wound renew
Of my Saviour crucified;
Let me share with thee His pain,
Who for all my sins was slain,
Who for me in torments died.

Christ, when Thou shalt call me hence,
Be Thy mother my defence,
Be Thy cross my victory;
While my body here decays,
May my soul Thy goodness praise,
Safe in paradise with Thee.

* * *

Five Minutes.
Fifth Mystery: The Crucifixion and Death of Our Lord.

O Good and Merciful Saviour! Thy love,
more than iron nails, keeps Thee riveted to
the cross, whereon Thou atonest for our sins
in the midst of unspeakable torments. We
find Thee also riveted by the same love in the
Sacrament of the altar, continuing Thy sacrifice to the end of ages in order to apply to us
the fruits thereof.

Sweet Lamb, perpetually immolated for us,
we adore Thee, and we beg of Thee, through
the intercession of Thy holy Mother, such a
hatred of sin as will make us prefer the death
of the body to the staining of the soul.

Recite slowly and devoutly the fifth decade. Then
ponder prayerfully over the following:

HAIL to Thee! true body sprung
From the Virgin Mary's womb!
The same that on the cross was hung,
And bore for man the bitter doom!

Thou Whose side was pierced and flowed
Both with water and with blood;
Suffer us to taste of Thee,
In our life's last agony.
O kind, O loving one!
O sweet Jesus, Mary's Son!

PRAYER TO THE EUCHARISTIC HEART
OF JESUS

O EUCHARISTIC Heart, O sovereign love of Our Lord Jesus, Who hast instituted the august Sacrament in order to dwell here below with us and to give to our souls Thy flesh as food and Thy blood as drink, we confidently trust, O Lord Jesus, in the supreme love which instituted the most holy Eucharist; and here, in the presence of this Victim, it is just that we should adore, confess and exalt this love, as the great storehouse of the life of Thy Church. This love is an urgent invitation for us, as though Thou didst say to us: "See how I love you! giving you My flesh as food, and My blood as drink; I desire by this union to excite your charity, I desire to unite you to Myself, I desire to effect the transformation of your souls into My crucified self, I Who am the bread of eternal life. Give Me, then, your hearts, live in My life, and you shall live in God."

We recognize, O Lord, that such is the appeal of Thy Eucharistic Heart, and we thank Thee for it, and we desire earnestly to respond to it. Grant us the grace to be keenly alive to this supreme love, with which, before Thy passion Thou didst invite us to receive and feed upon Thy sacred body. Print deeply on our souls the firm determination to respond faithfully to this invitation. Give us devotion and reverence whereby we may honor and receive worthily the gift of Thy supreme love, and of Thy Eucharistic Heart.

Grant that we may thus be able, with Thy grace, to celebrate profitably the remembrance of Thy passion, to make reparation for our offences and our coldness, to nourish and increase our love for Thee, and to keep ever living in our hearts this seed of a blessed immortality. Amen.

(Indulgence of 300 days during Exposition)

Talk familiarly with Jesus and make an act of Spiritual Communion.

PRINTED BY BENZIGER BROTHERS, NEW YORK

CPSIA information can be obtained
at www.ICGtesting.com
Printed in the USA
BVHW041120131221
623919BV00007B/255